MFC Doodles Book,

For relaxing

AF351639

This book belongs to

____

Maud Feral-Chauveau

*I will be really happy to see your colors and to share with you,
also join me on my Facebook page.
See you soon*

*https://www.facebook.com/MFC-Peinture-graphisme-
illustrations*

*Other books by the same author
(availbale on Amazon and Book Depository)
- The feet in the water
- A pencil on the heart
- Color your Kimmidoll
- Back to the sea*

*Je serais ravie de voir vos mises en couleurs et de partager avec vous
dans la convivialité,
alors rejoignez moi sur ma page Facebook.
À bientôt*

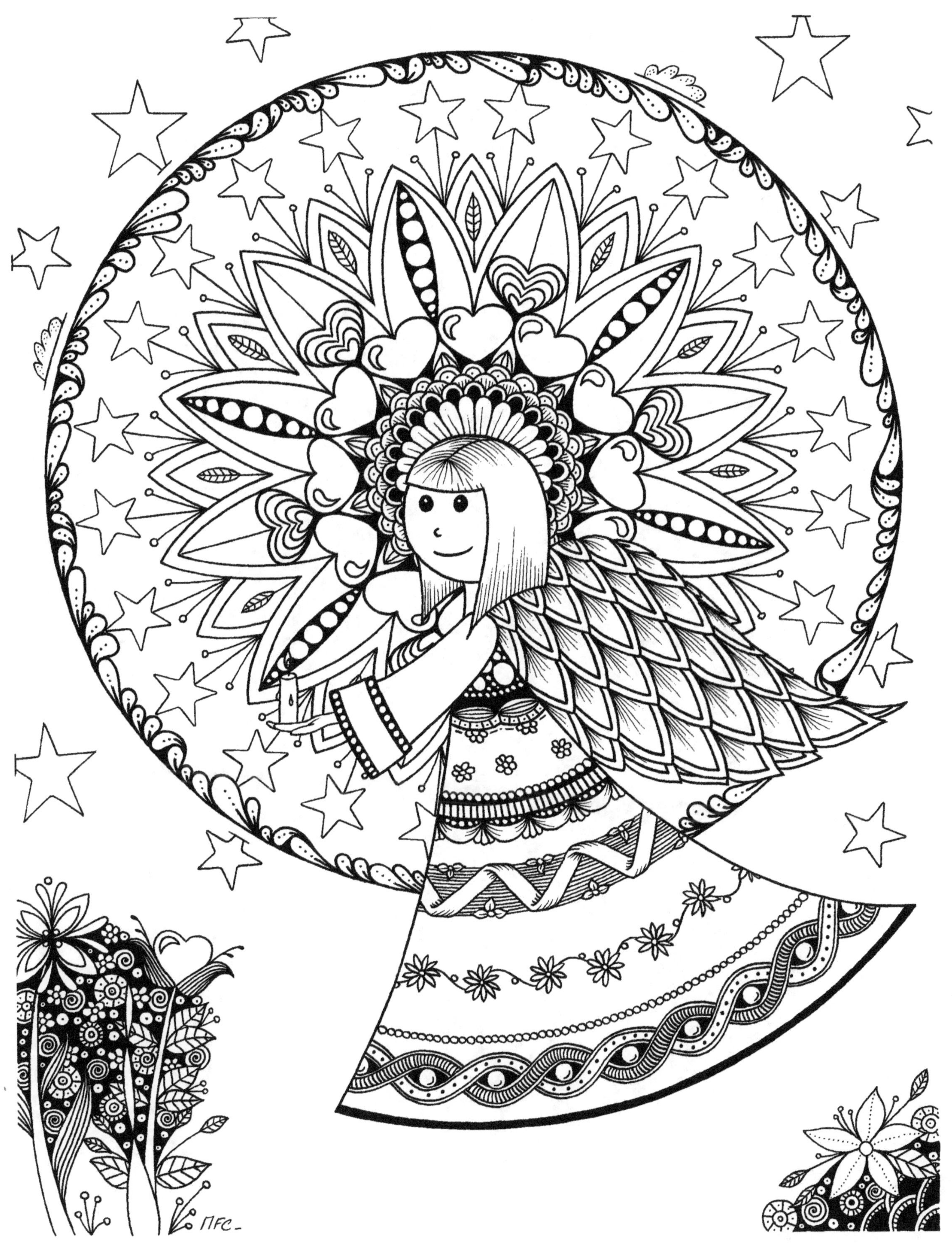

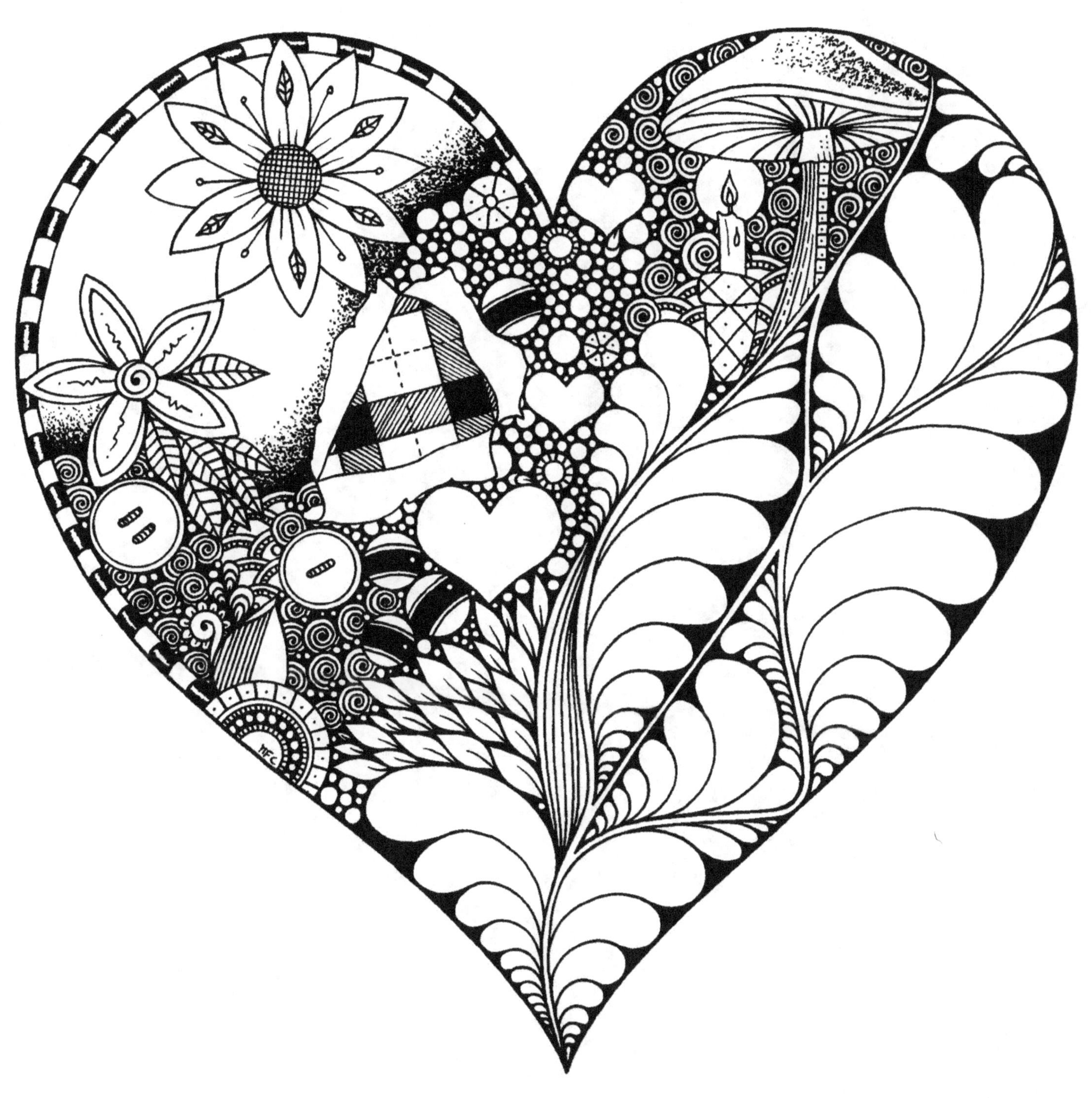

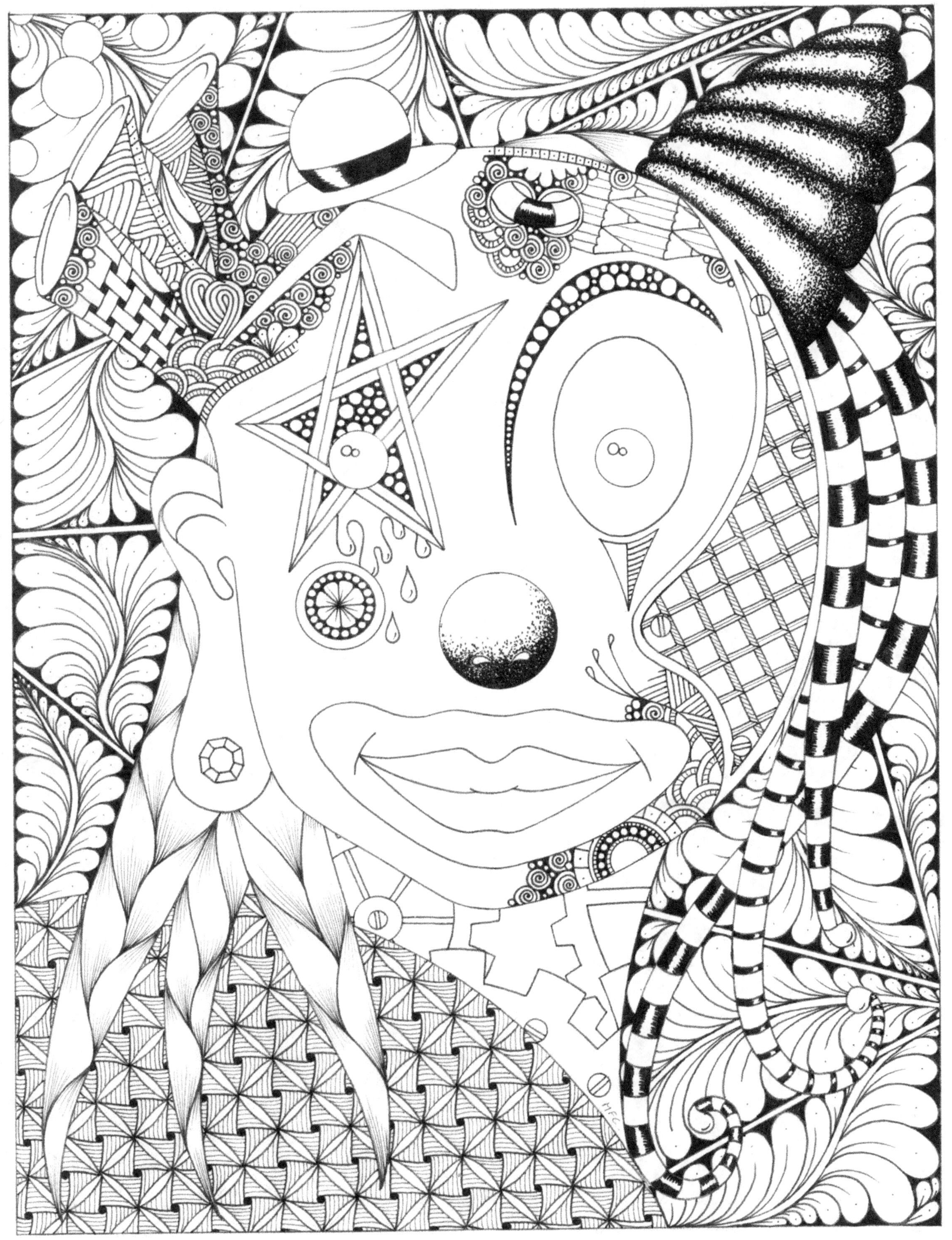

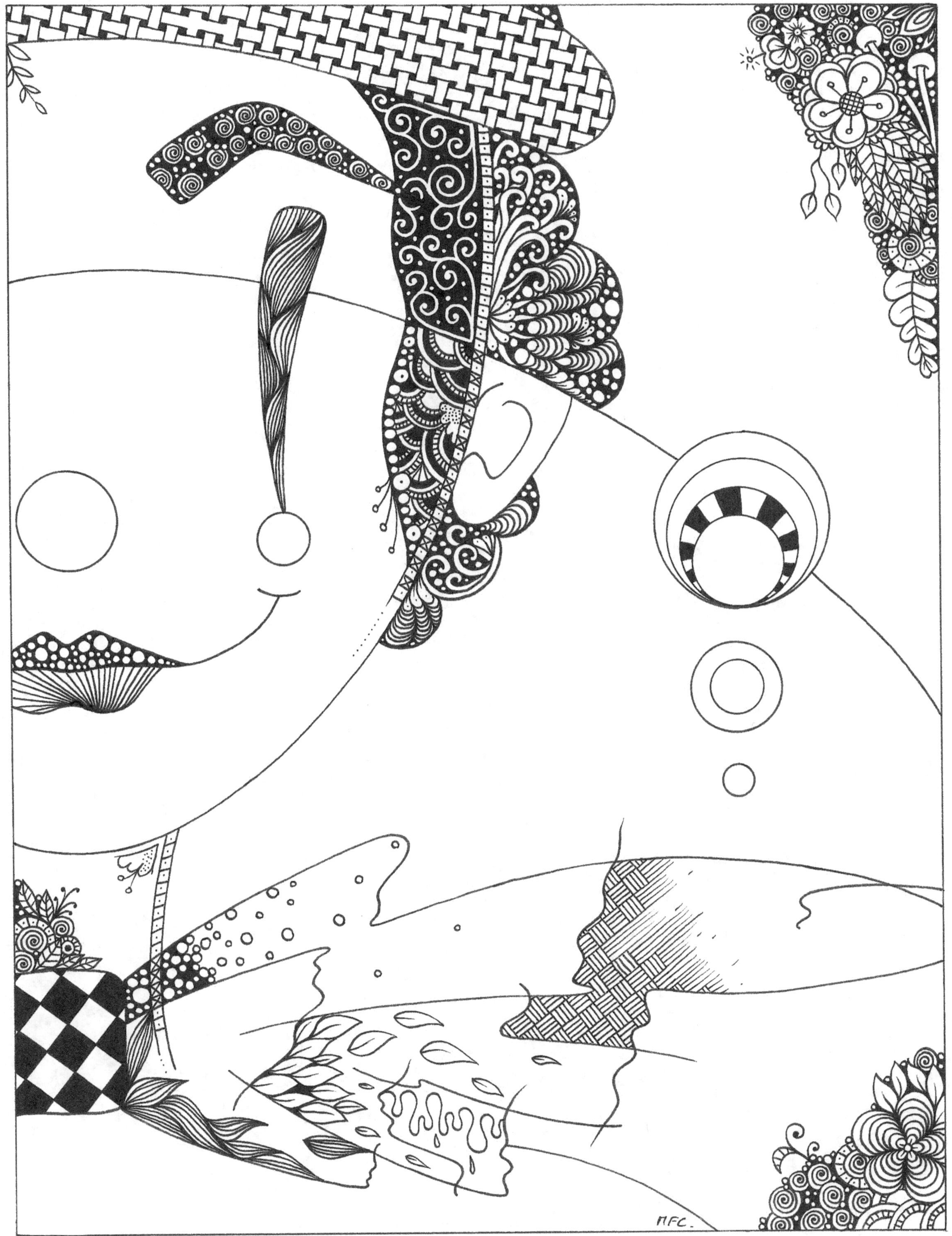

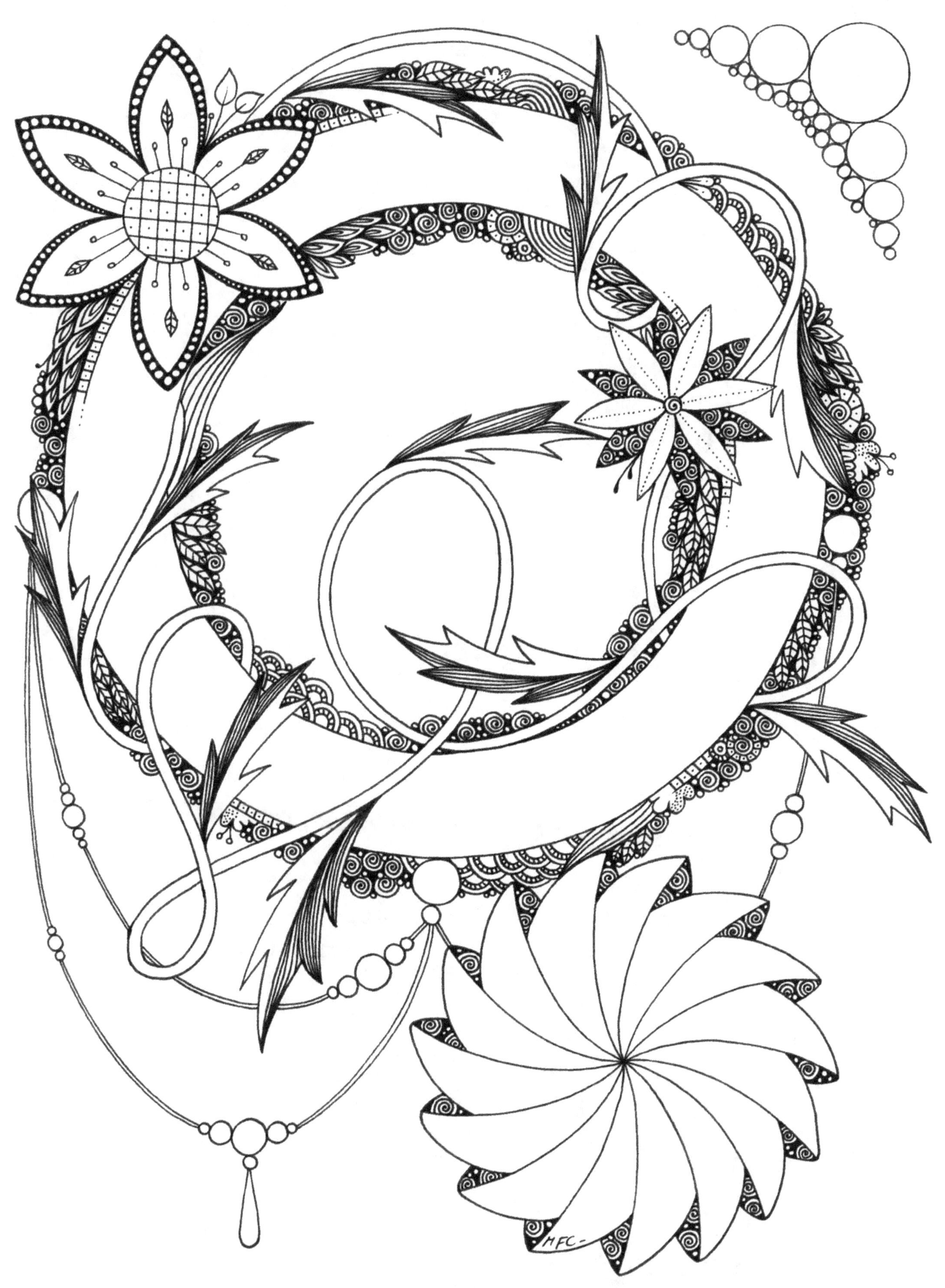

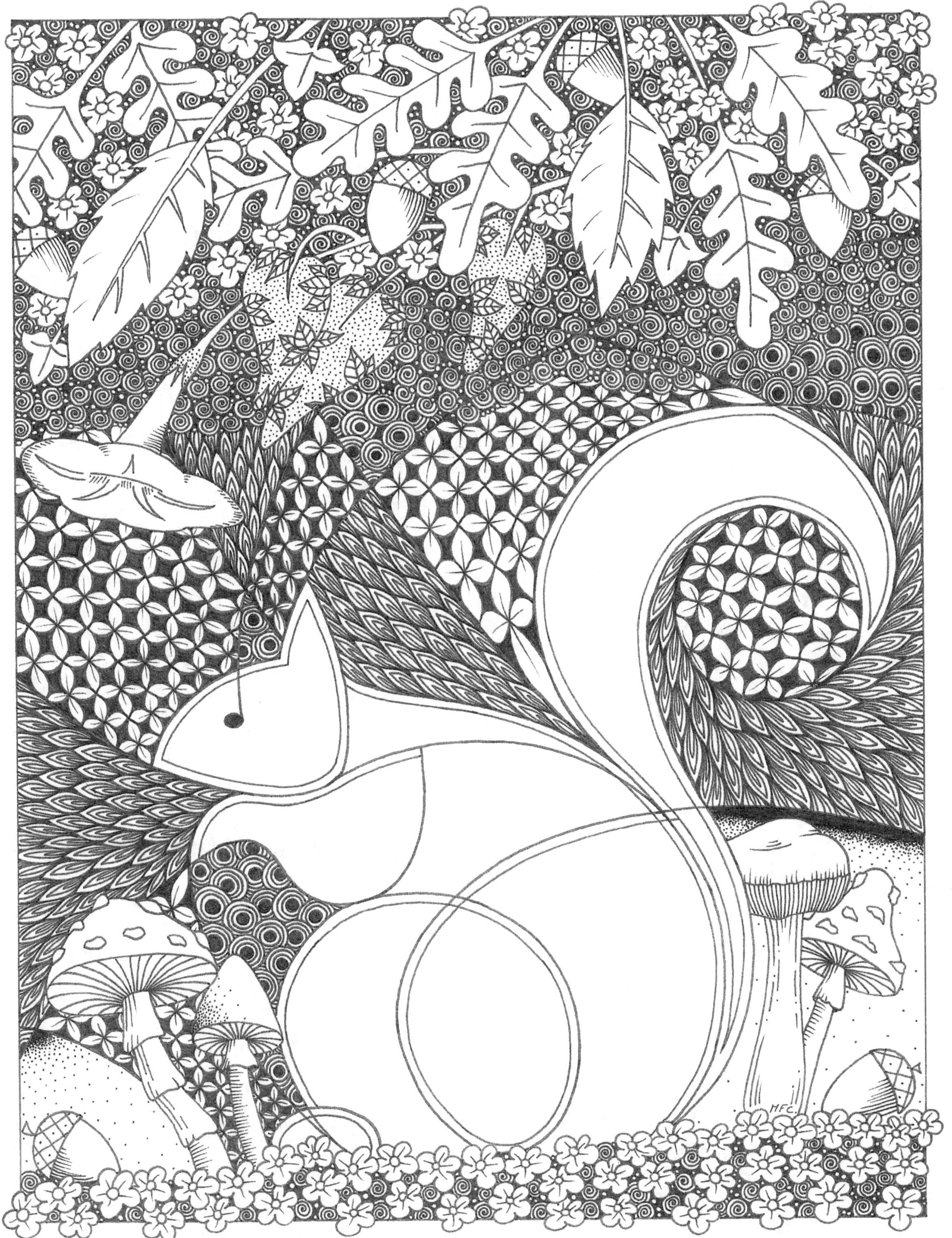

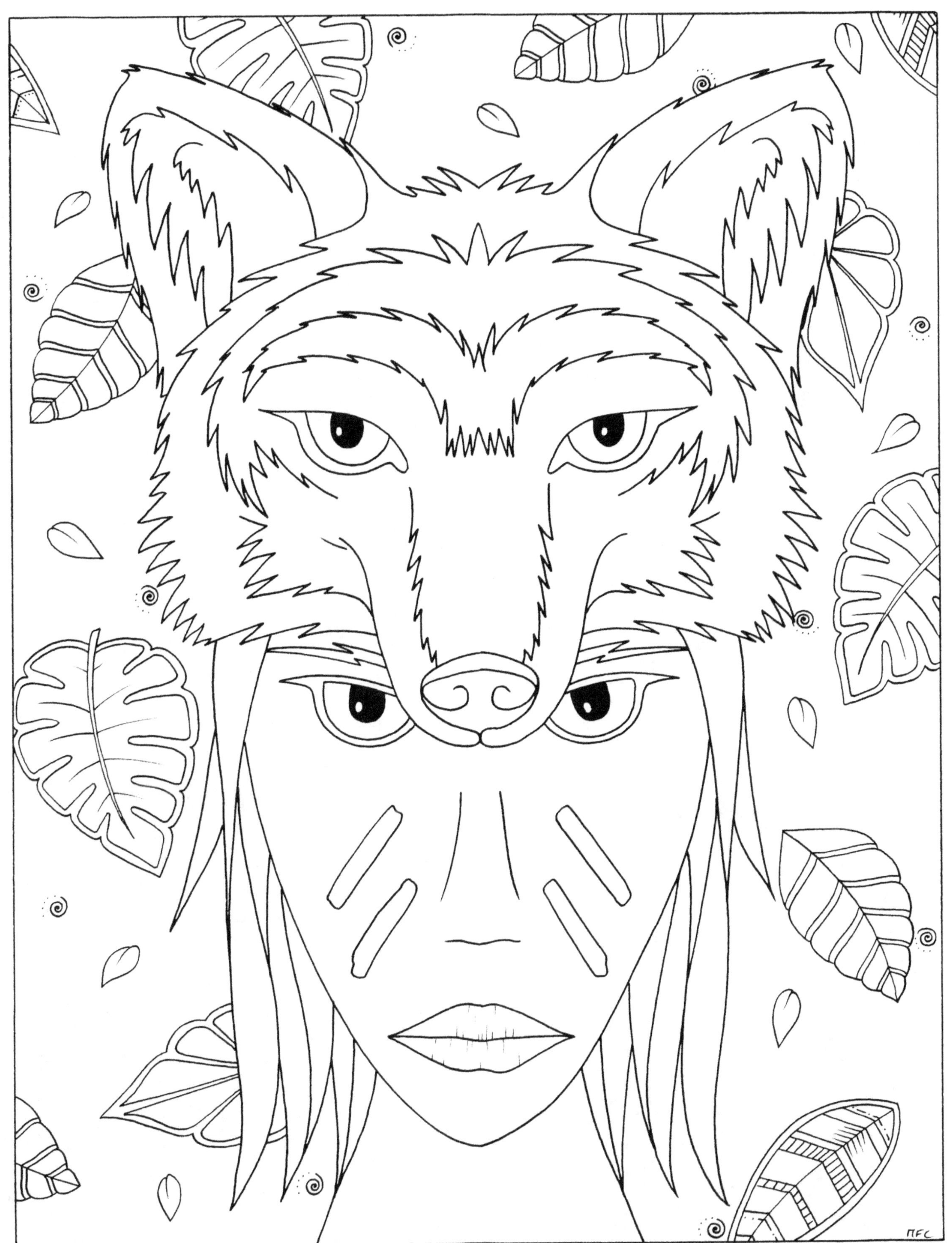

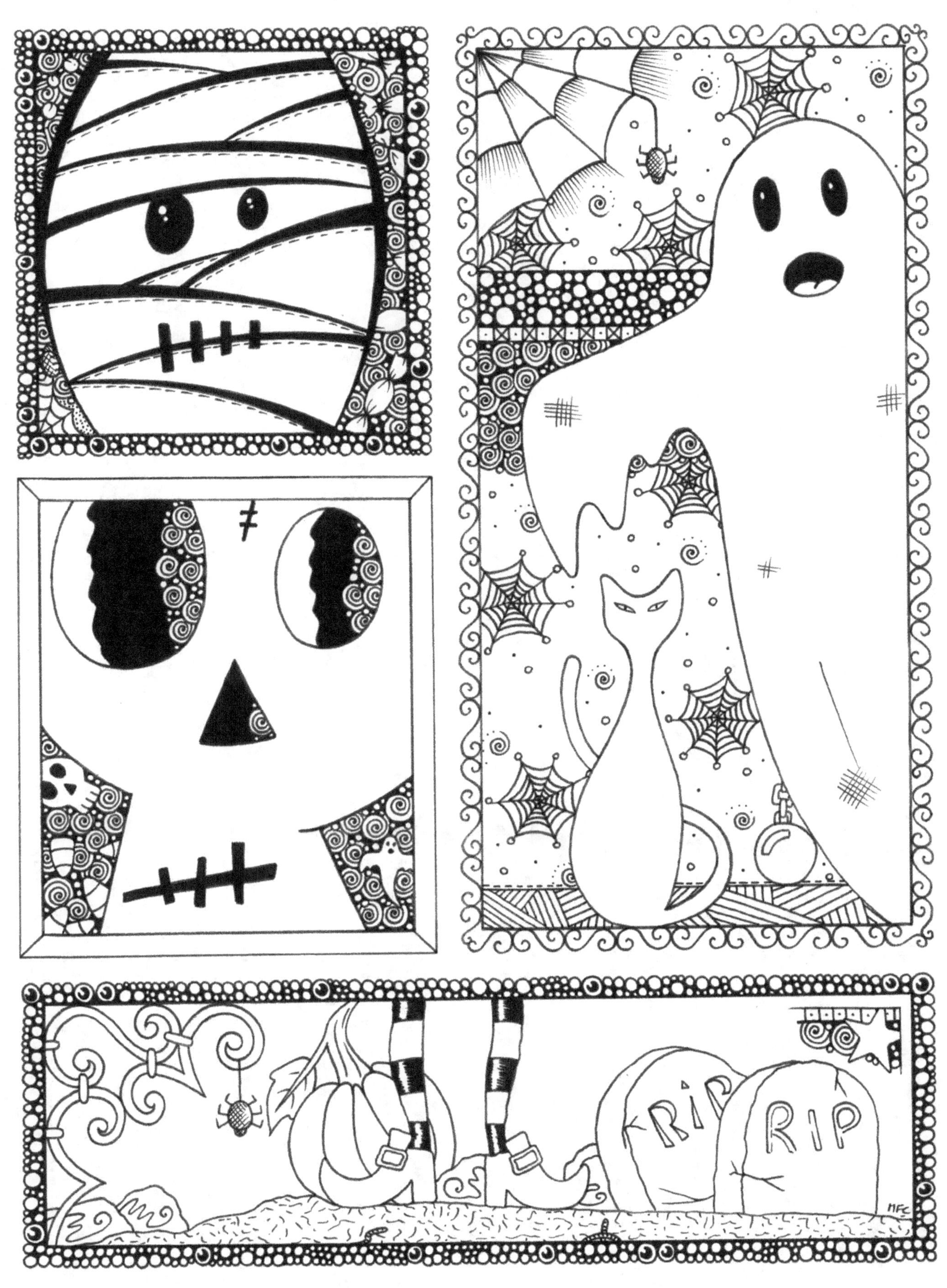

RIP
RIP

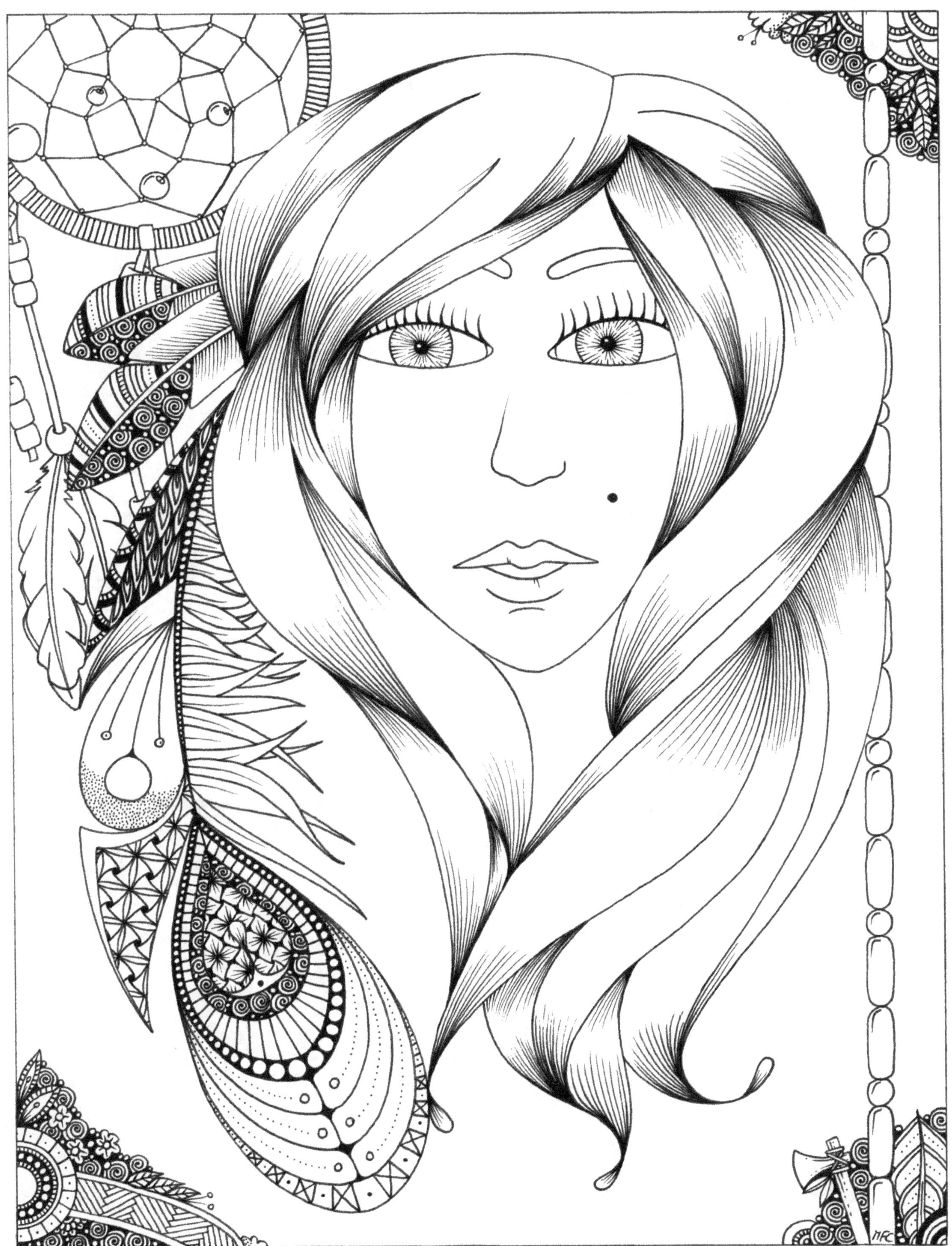

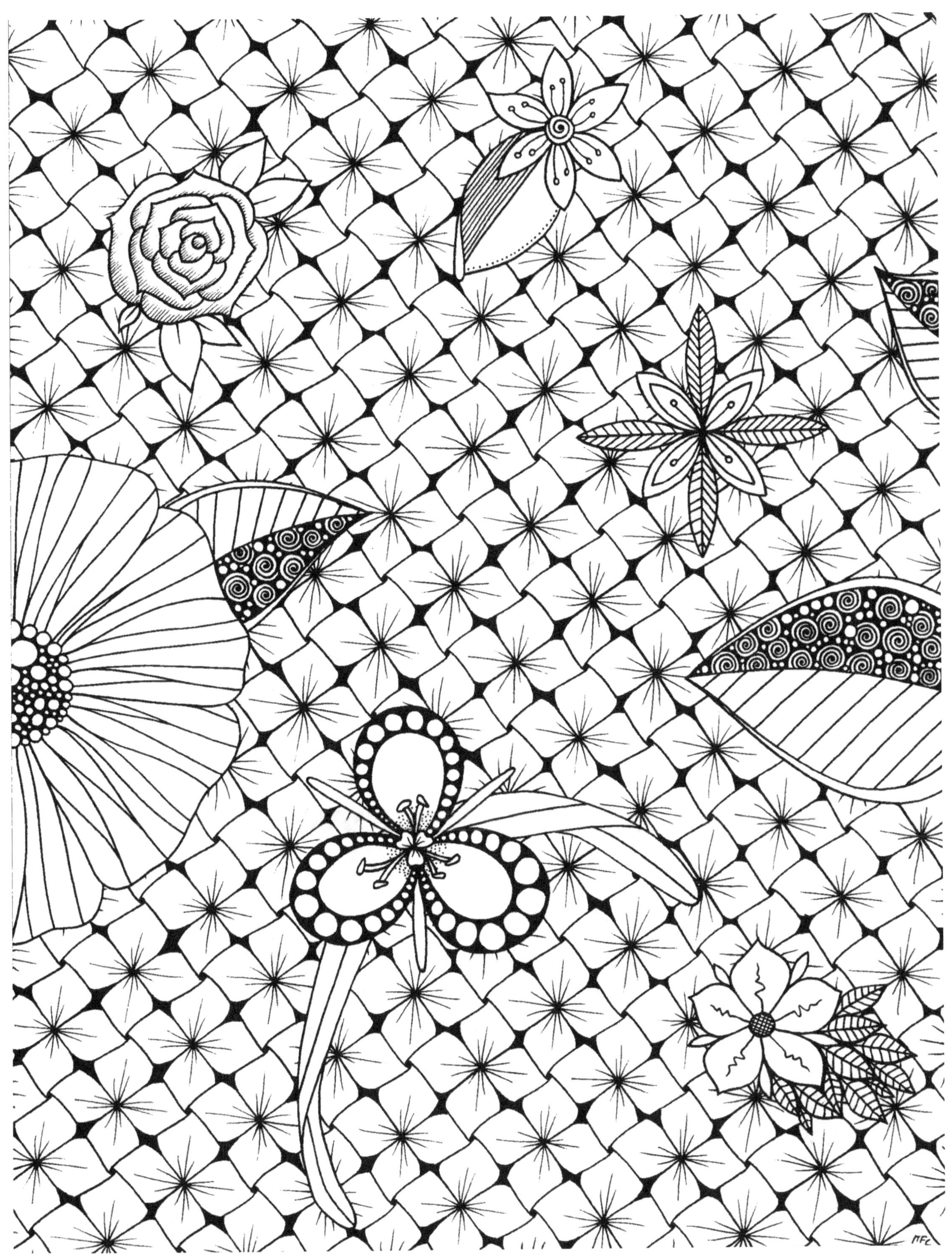

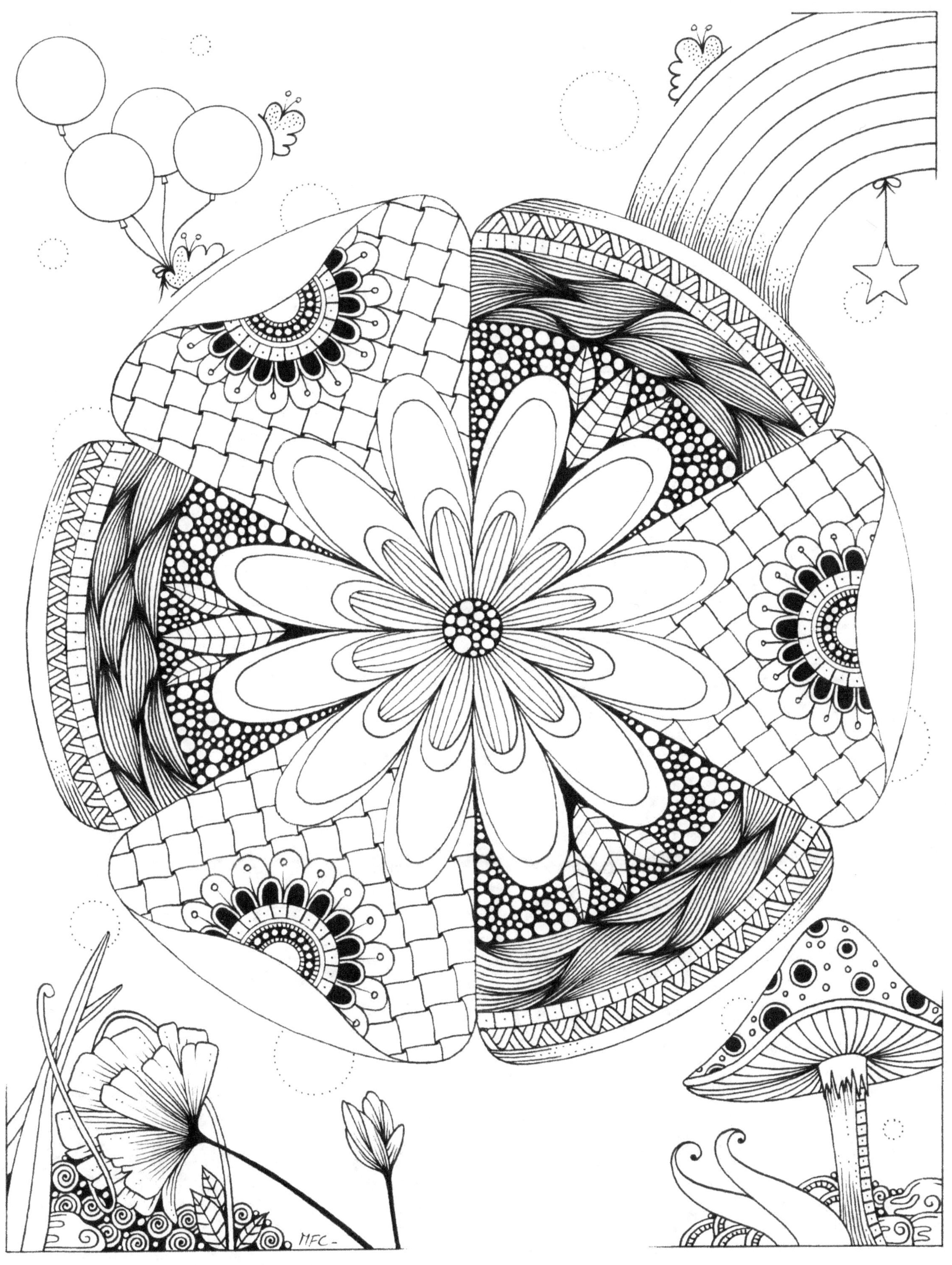

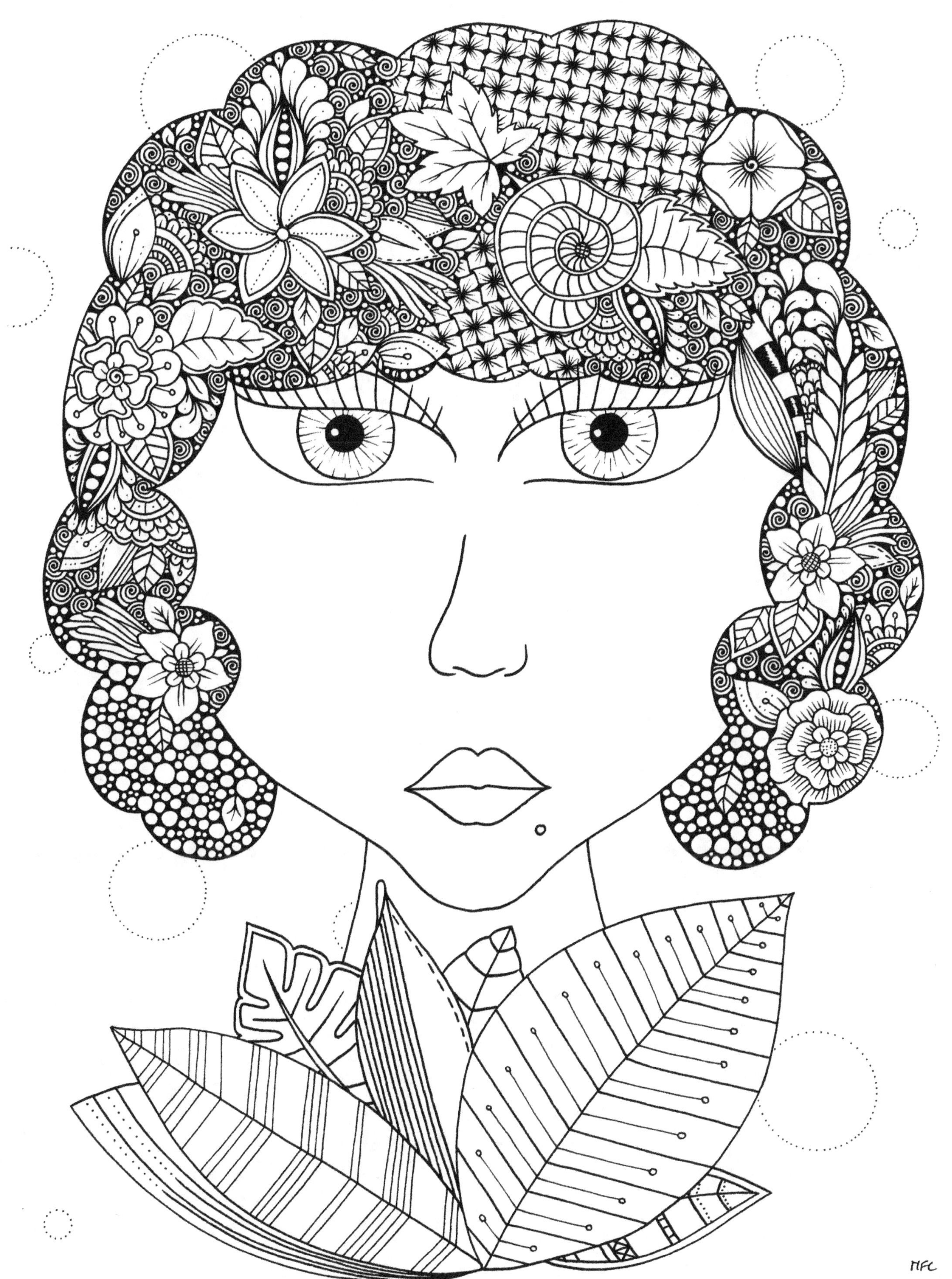

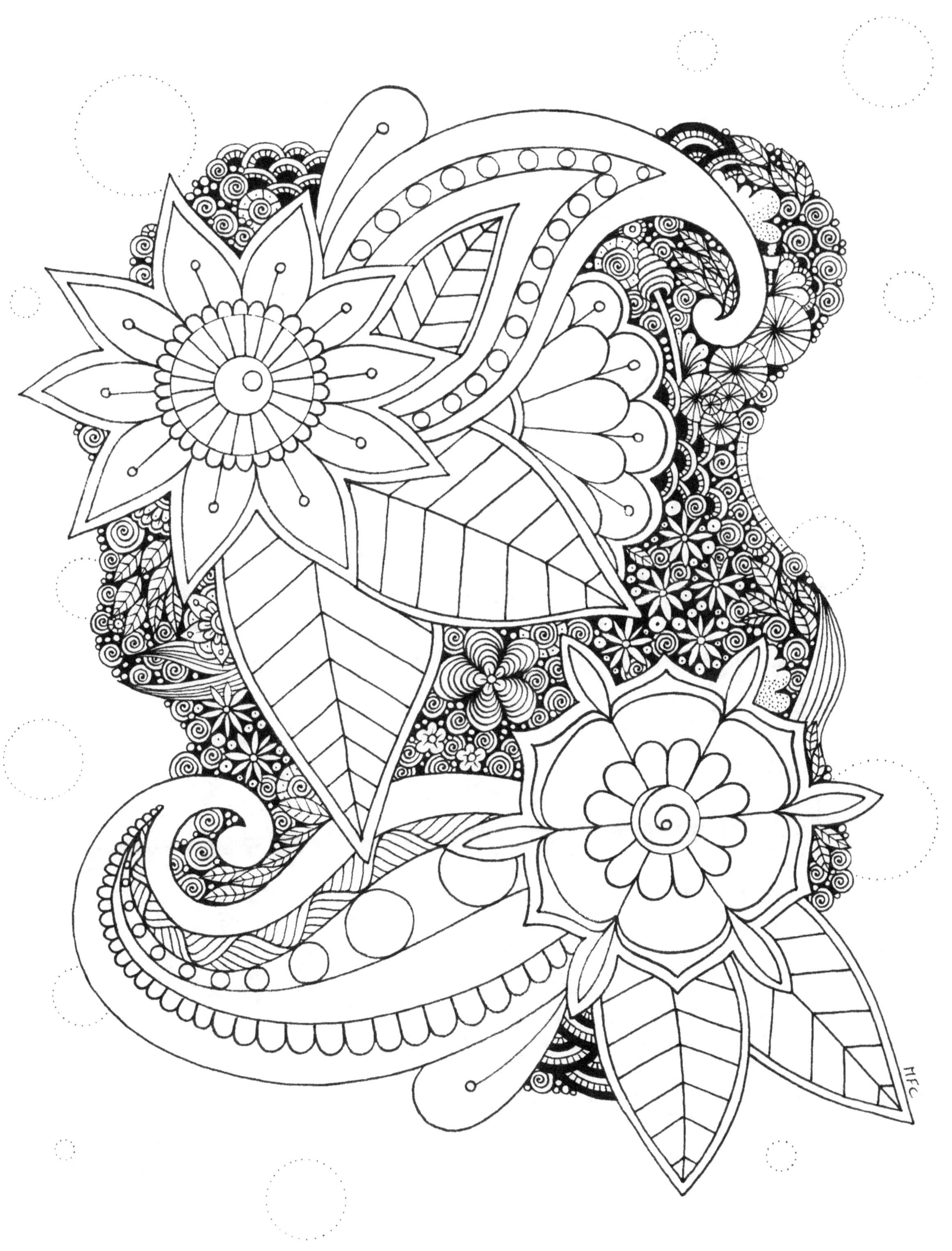

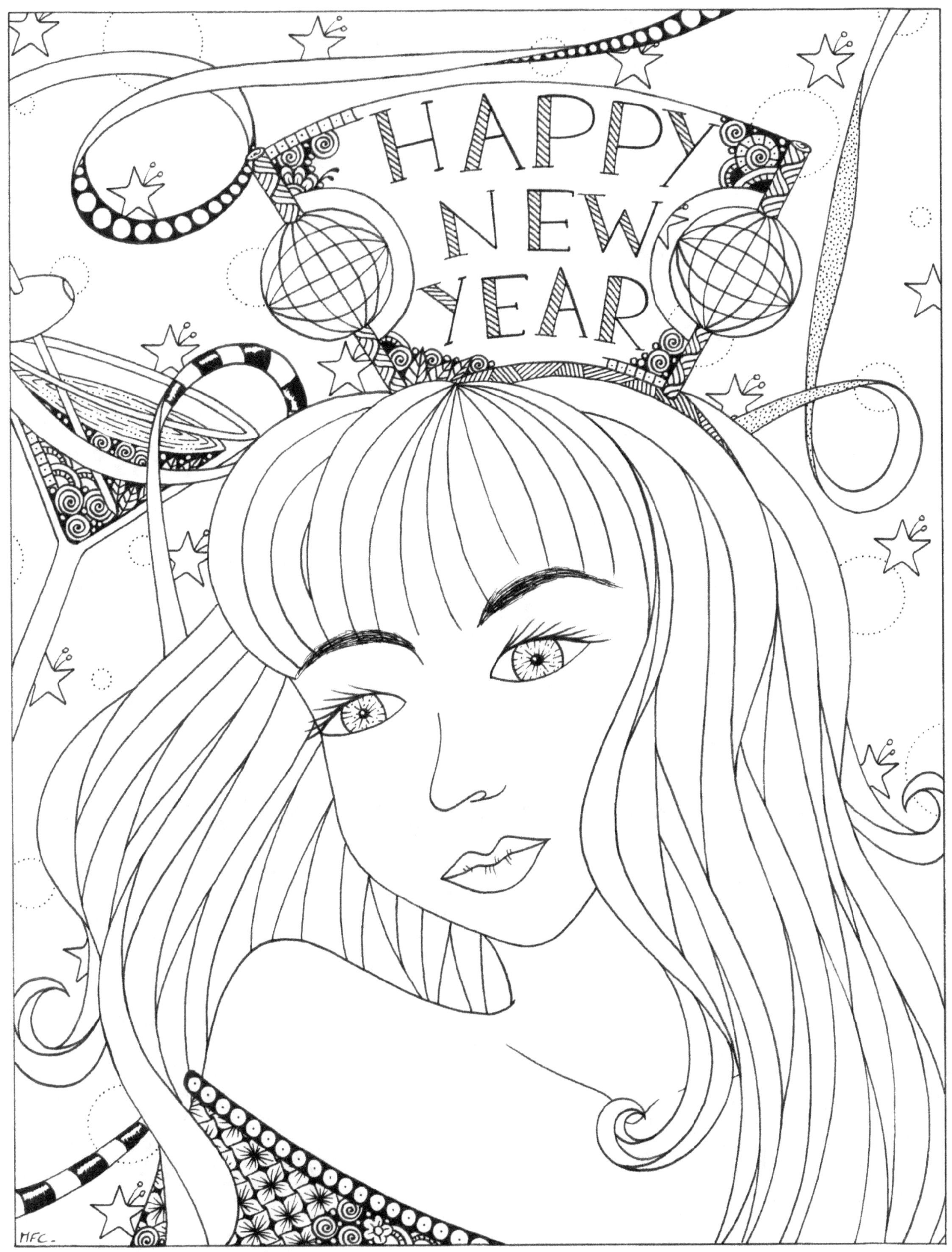

HAPPY
NEW
YEAR
MFC.

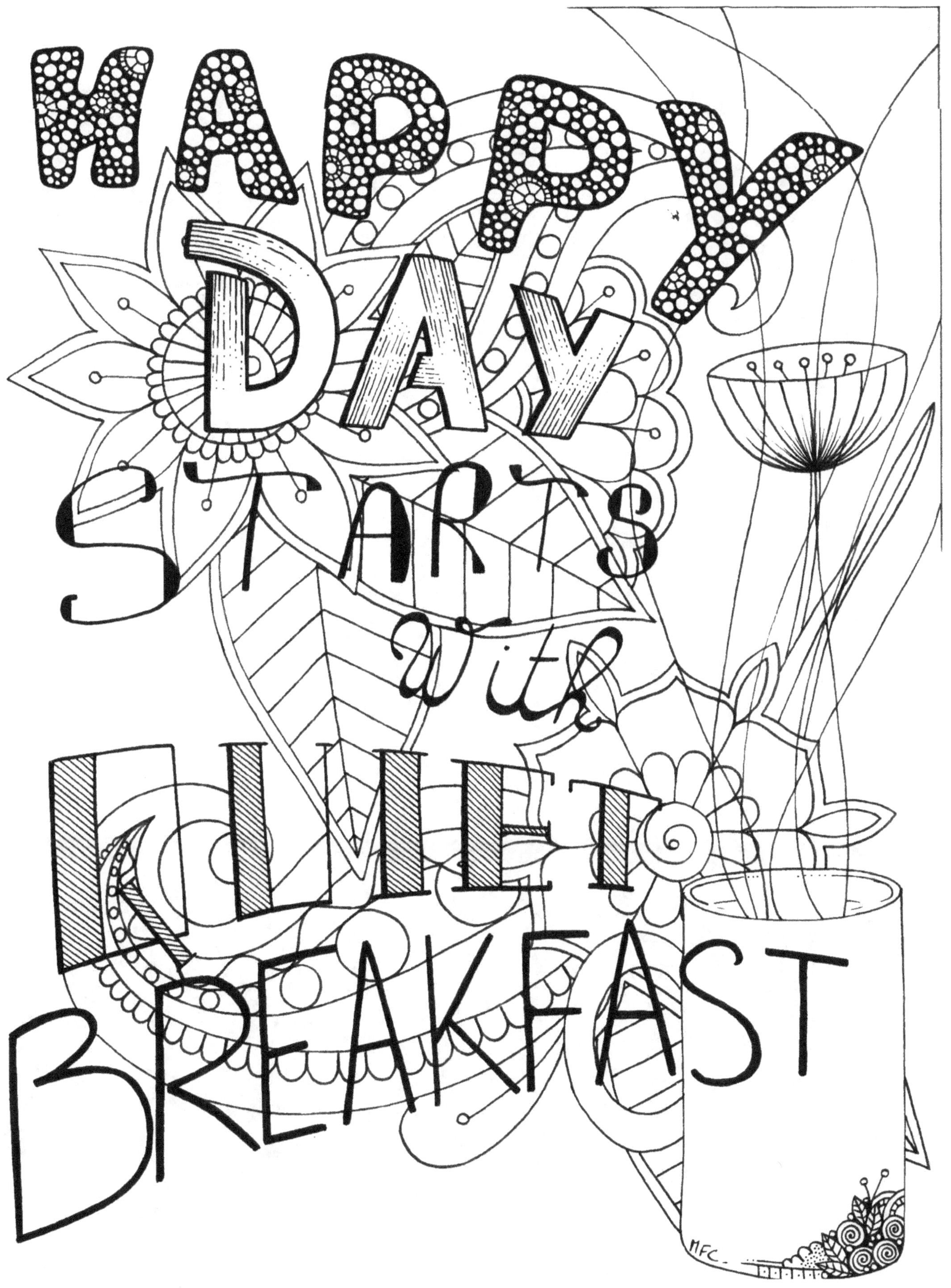

HAPPY
DAY
STARTS
with
QUIET
BREAKFAST
MFC

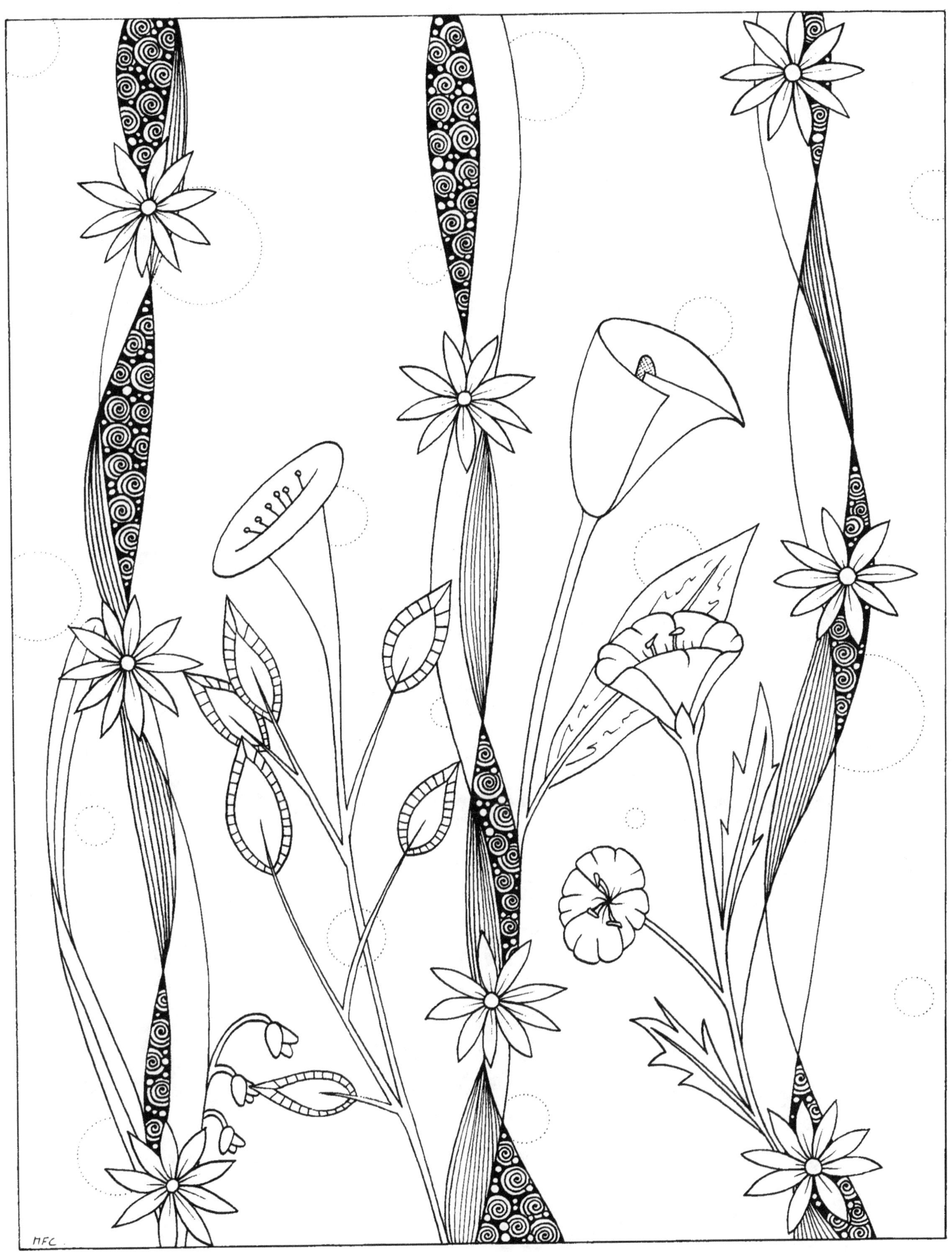
MFC

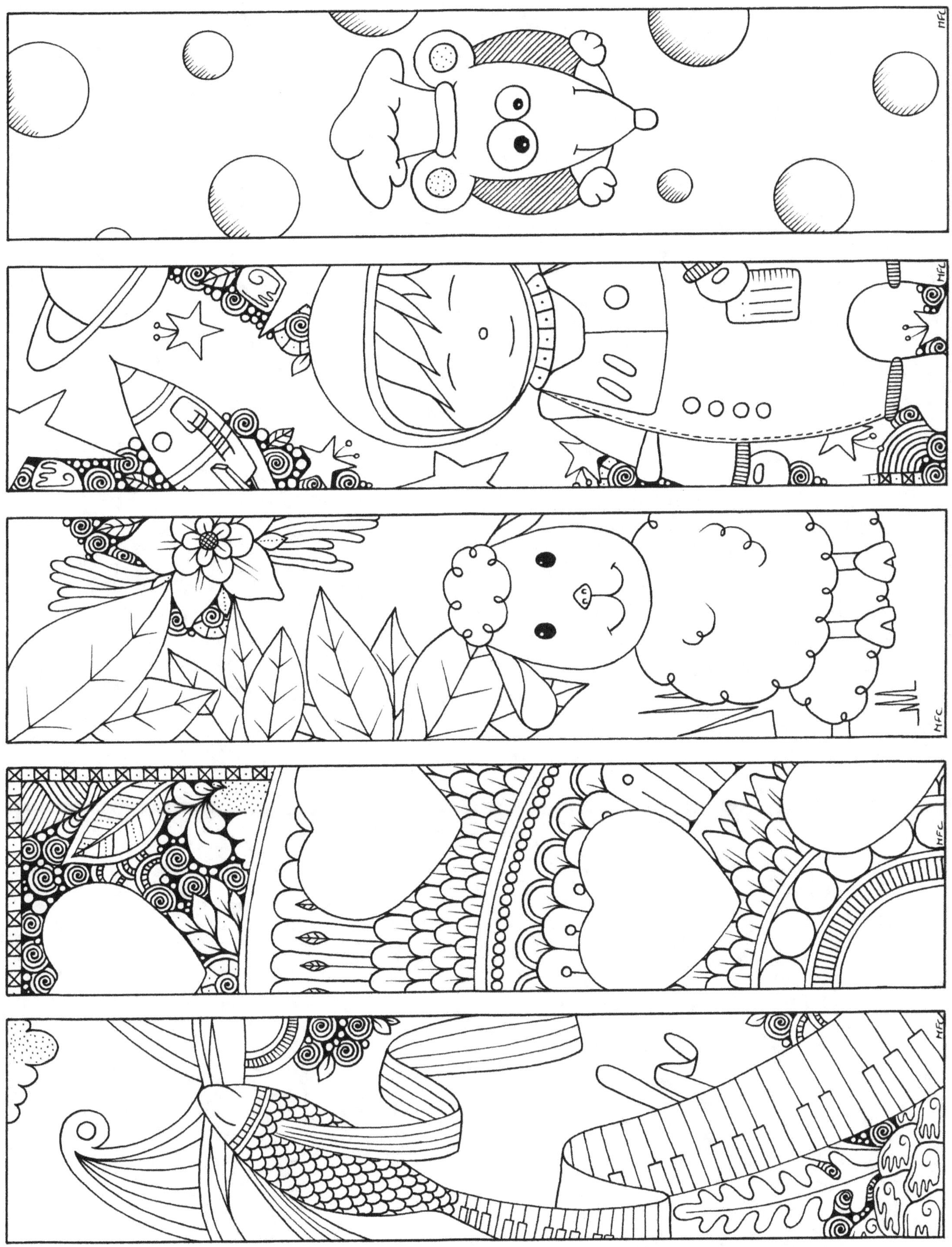

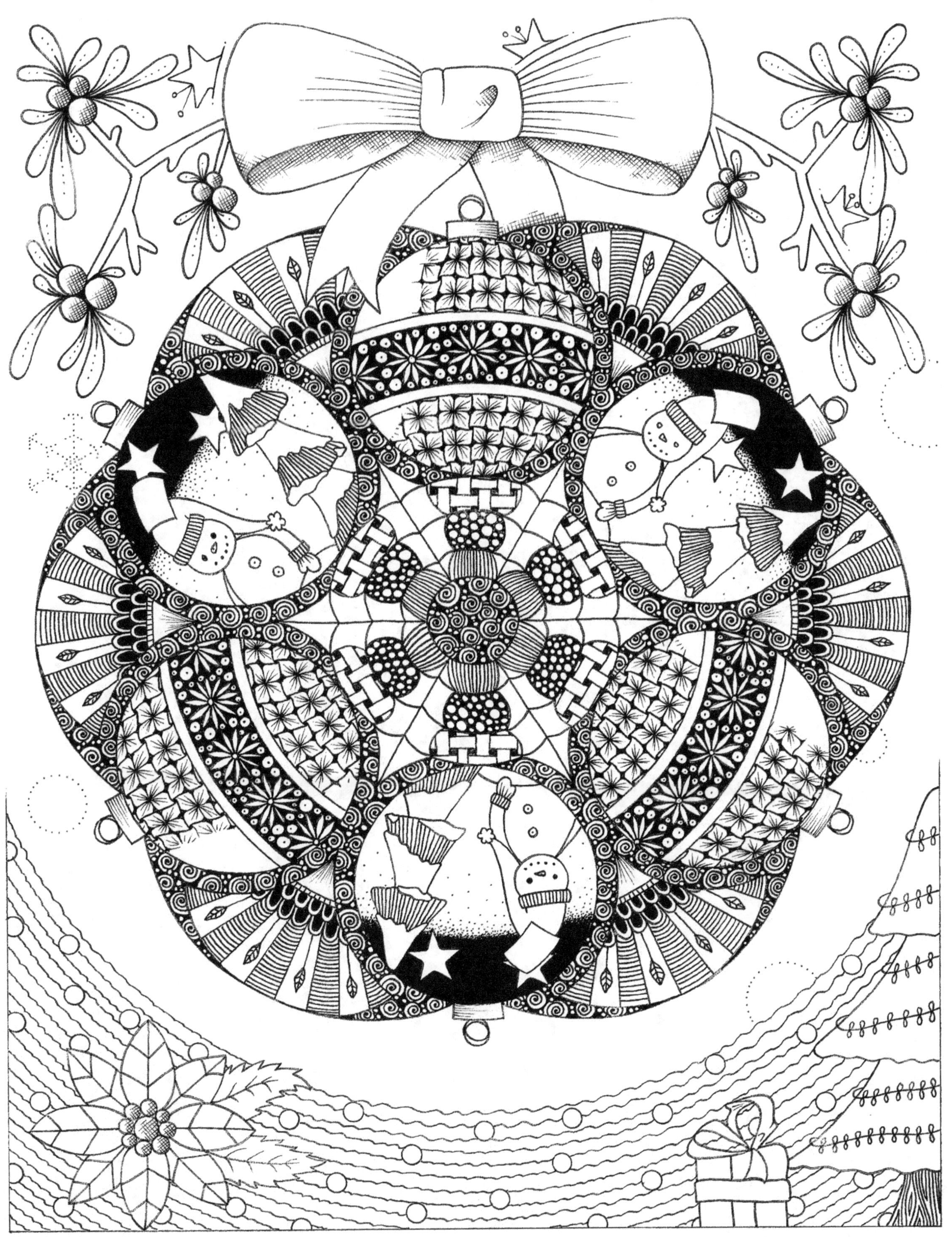

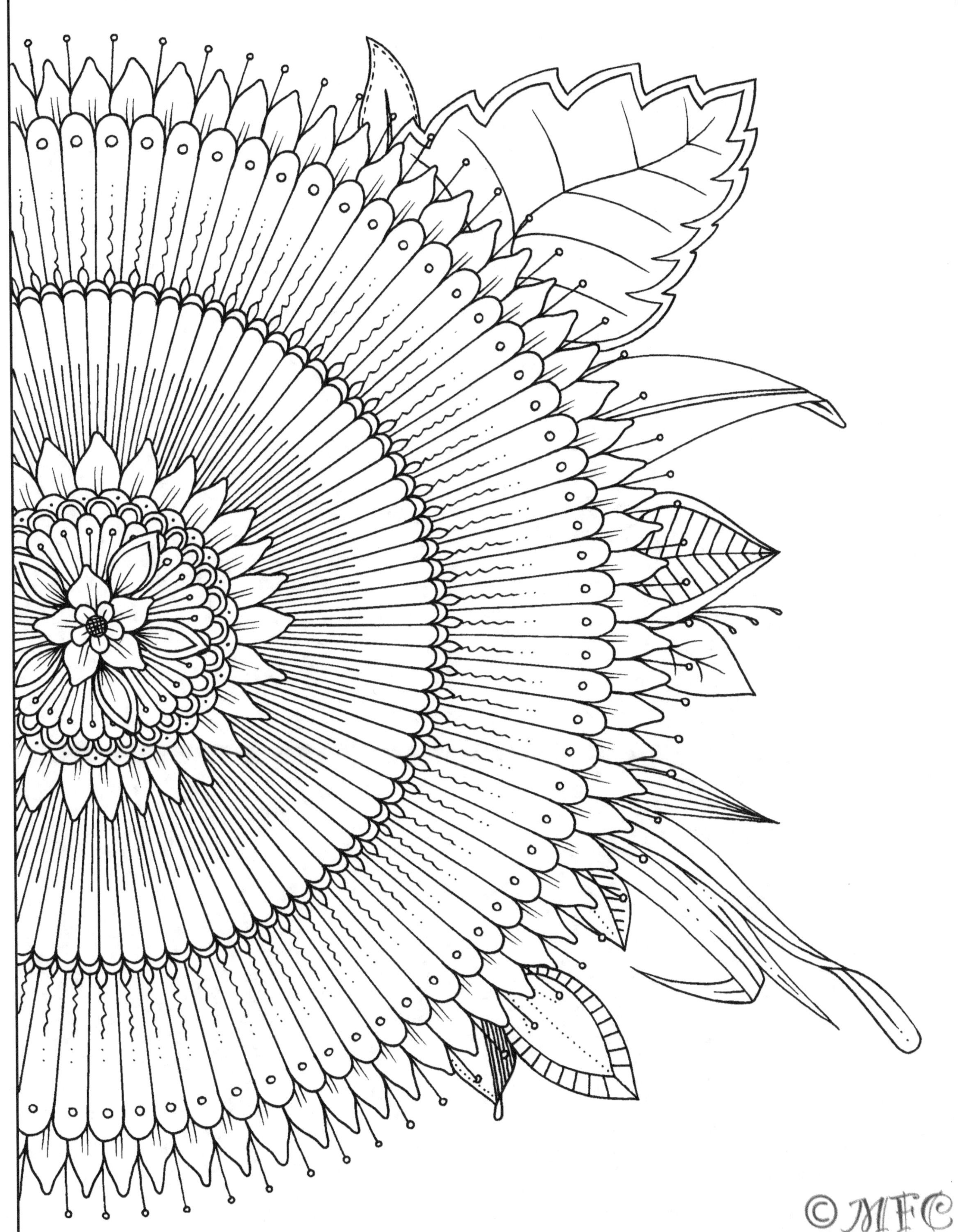
©MFC

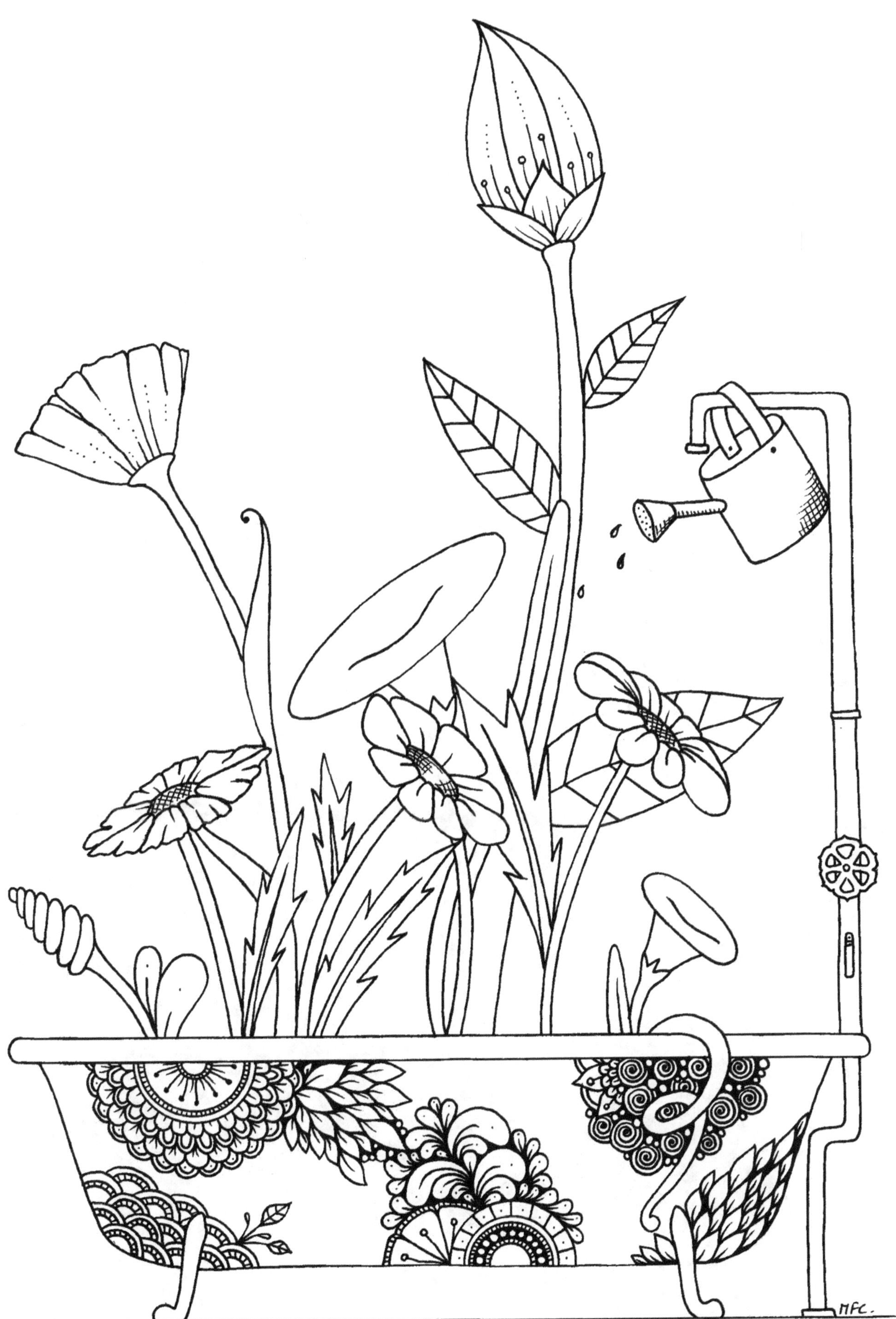

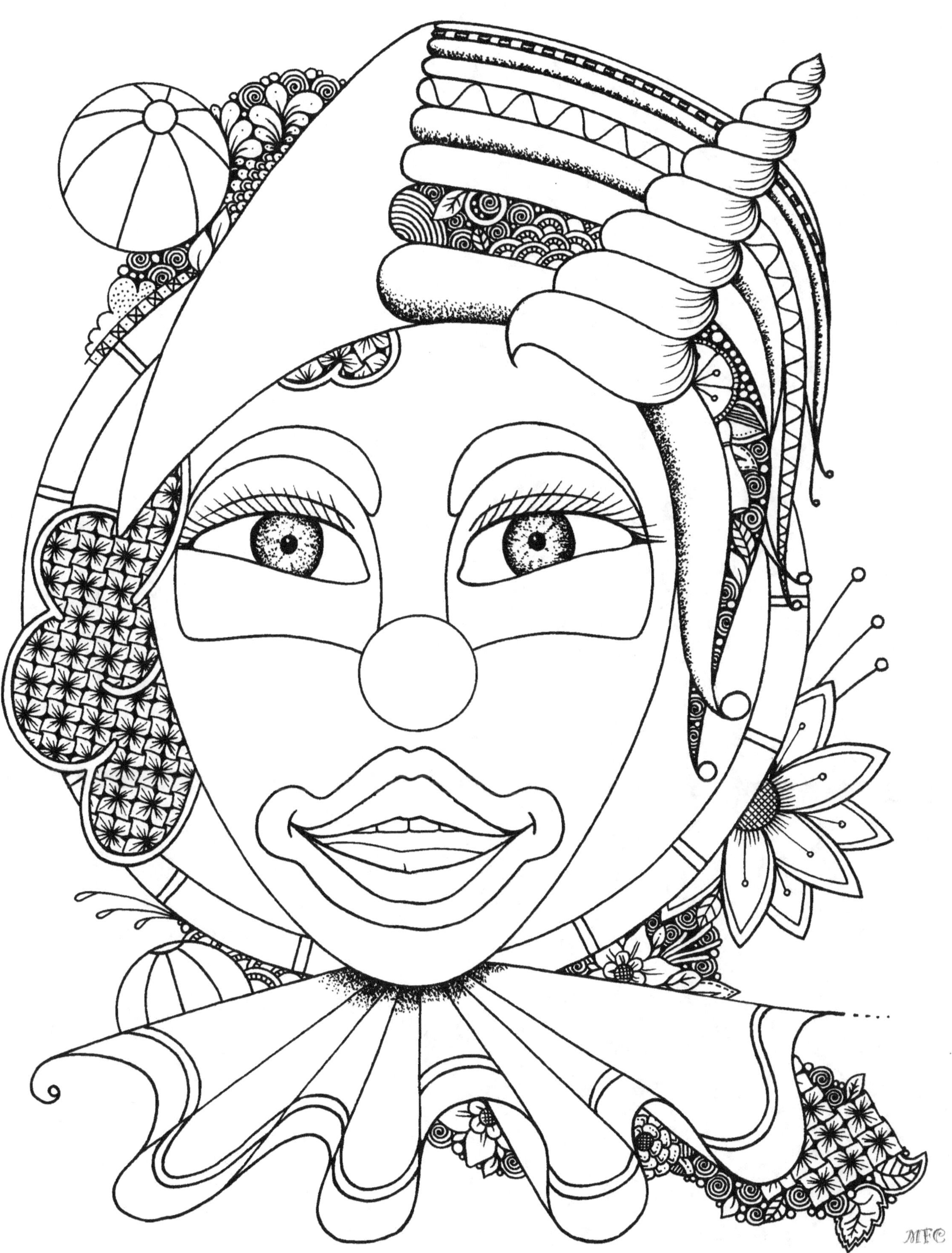

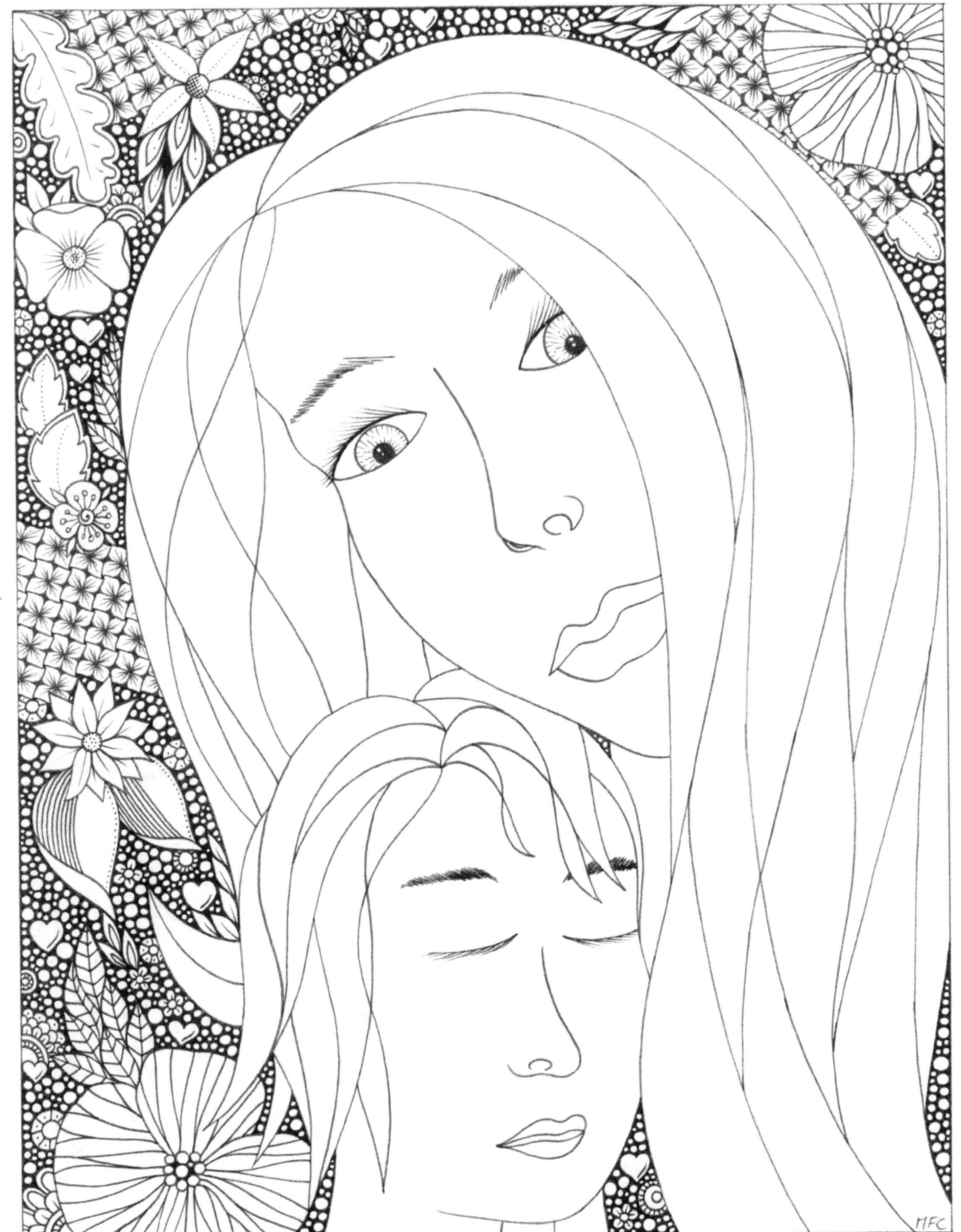
MFC

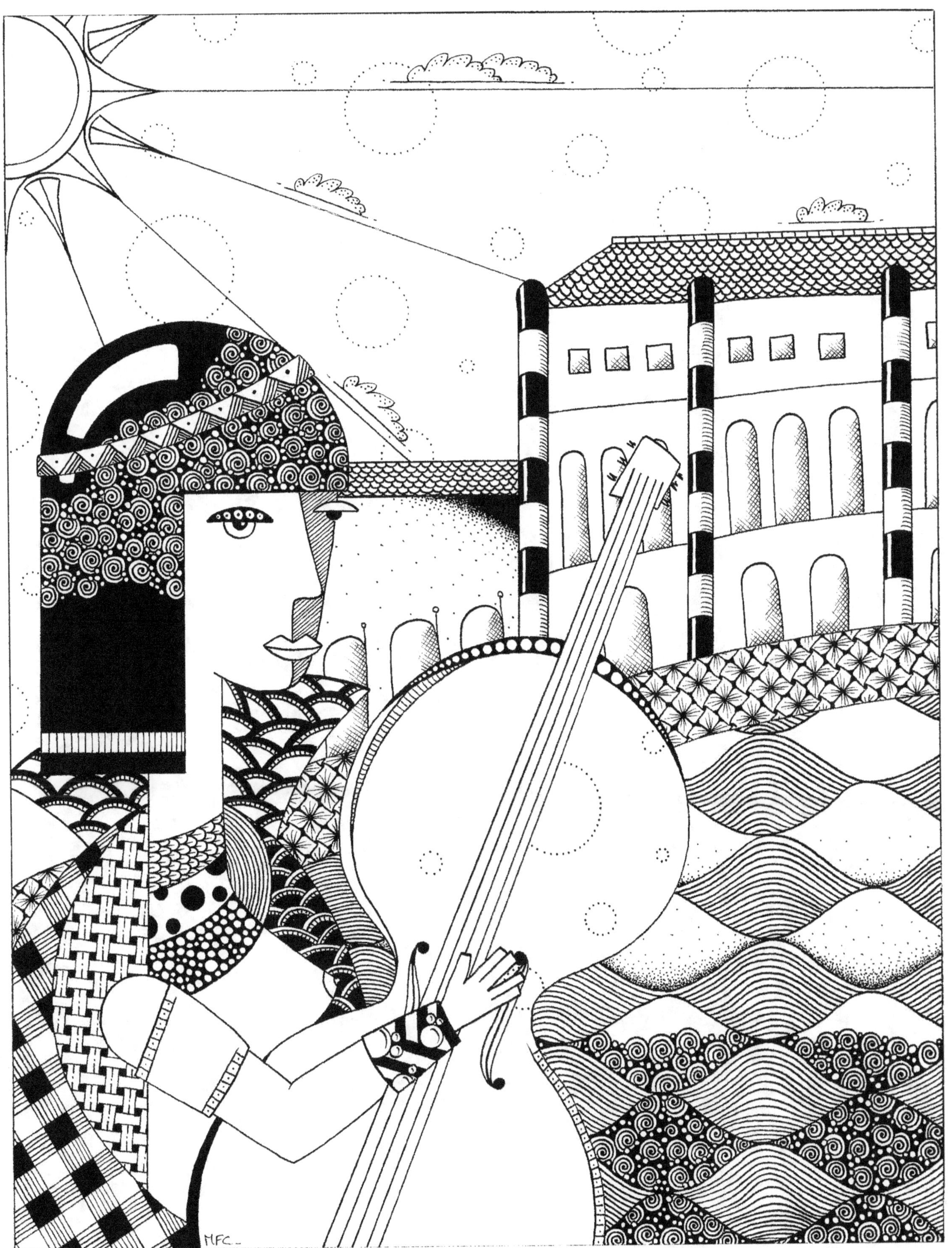

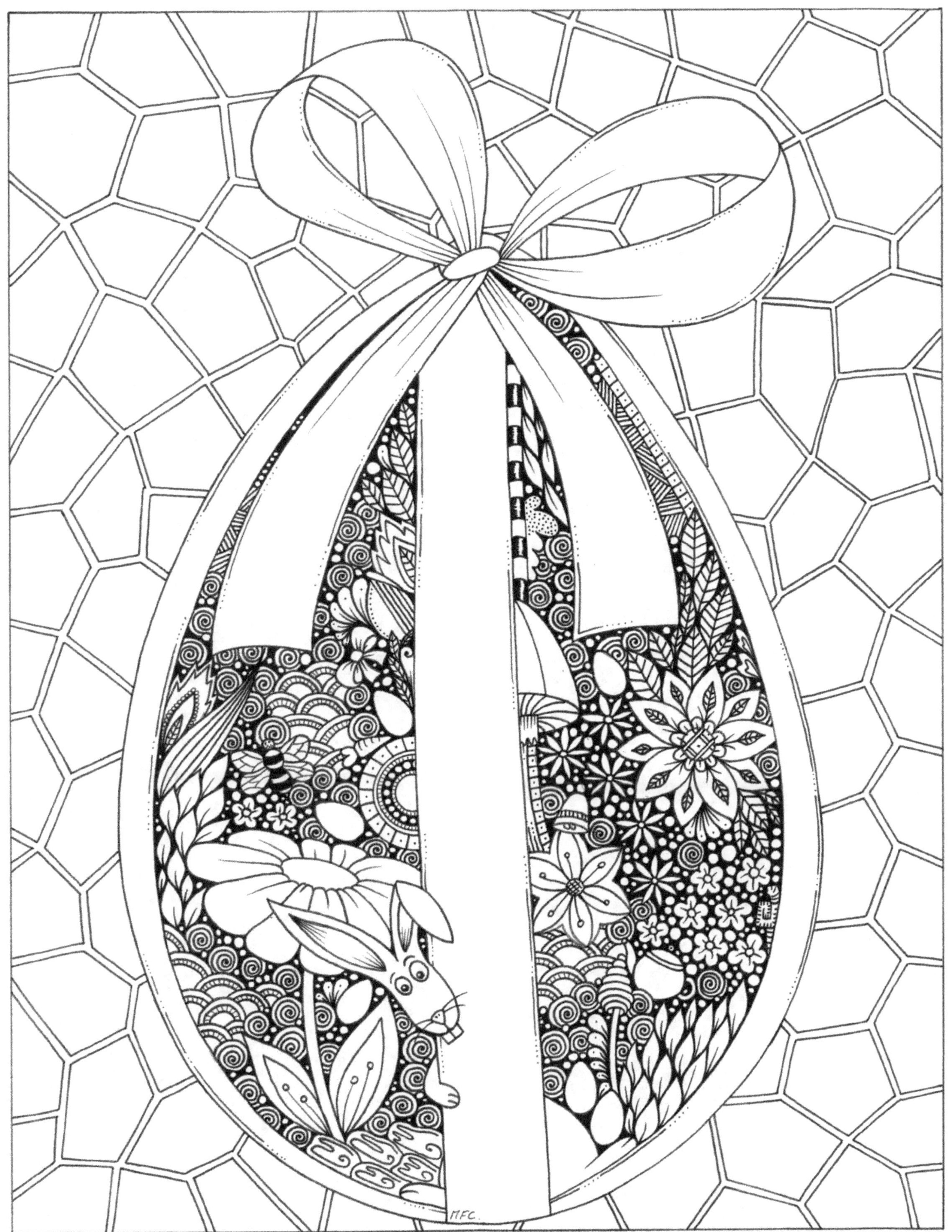

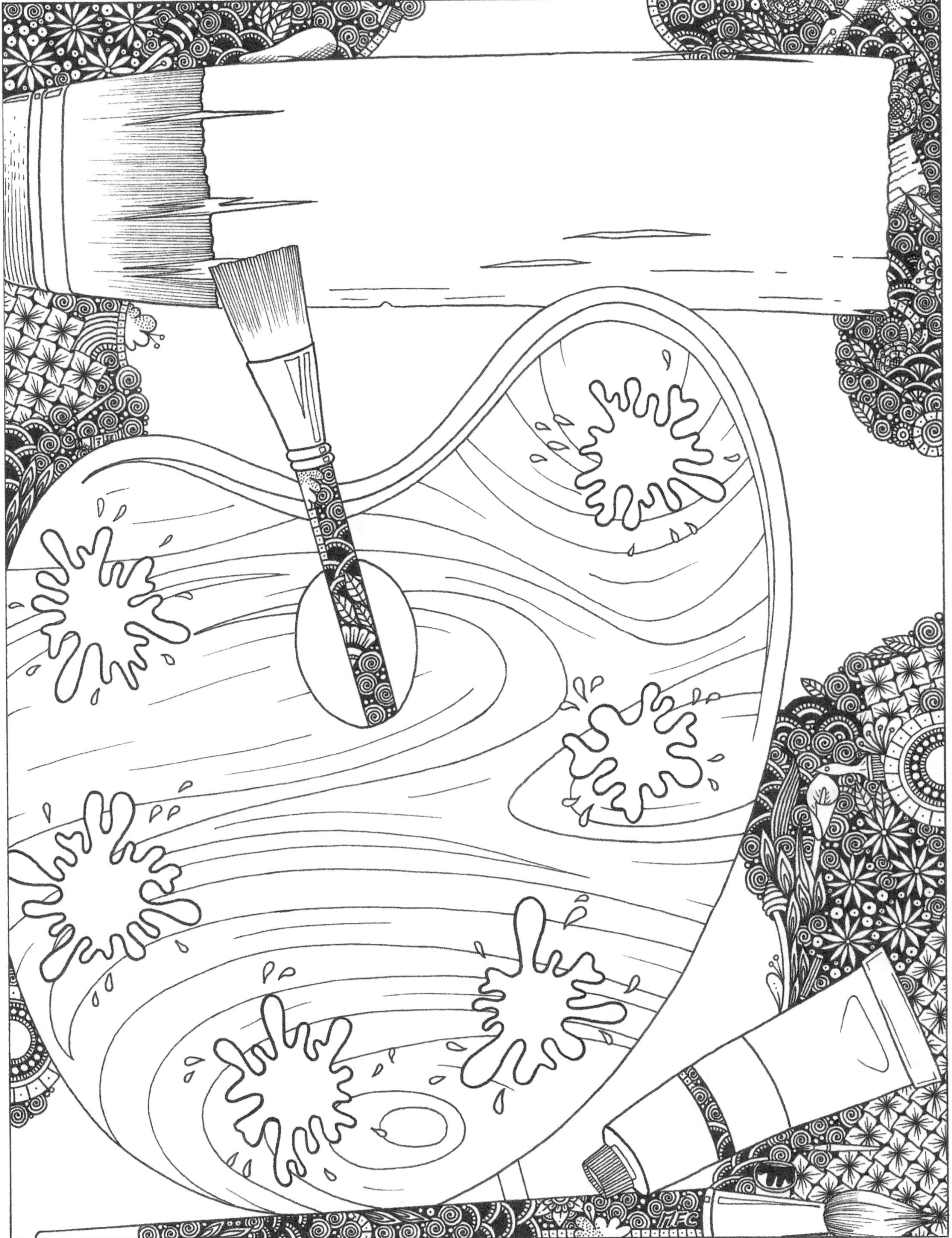

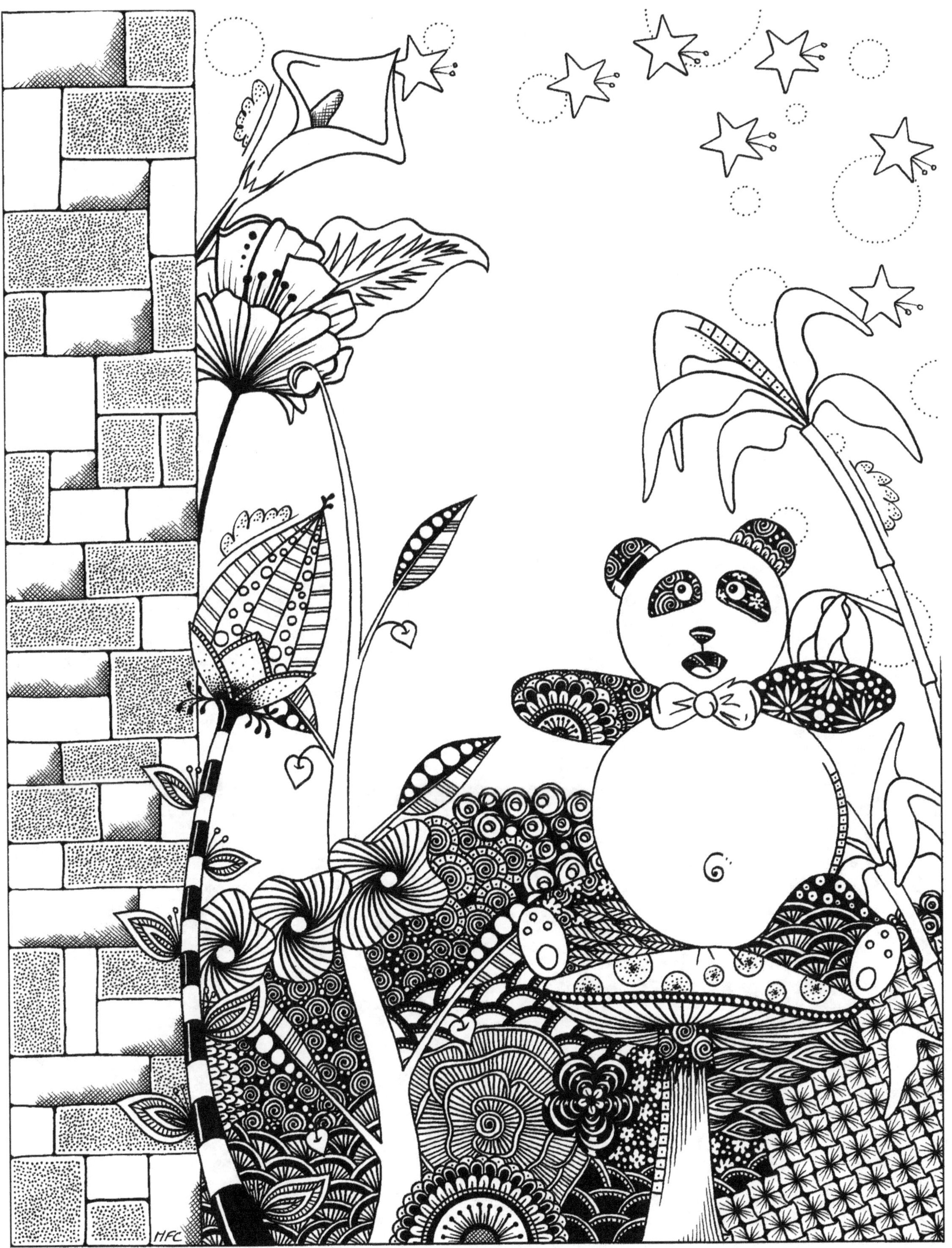

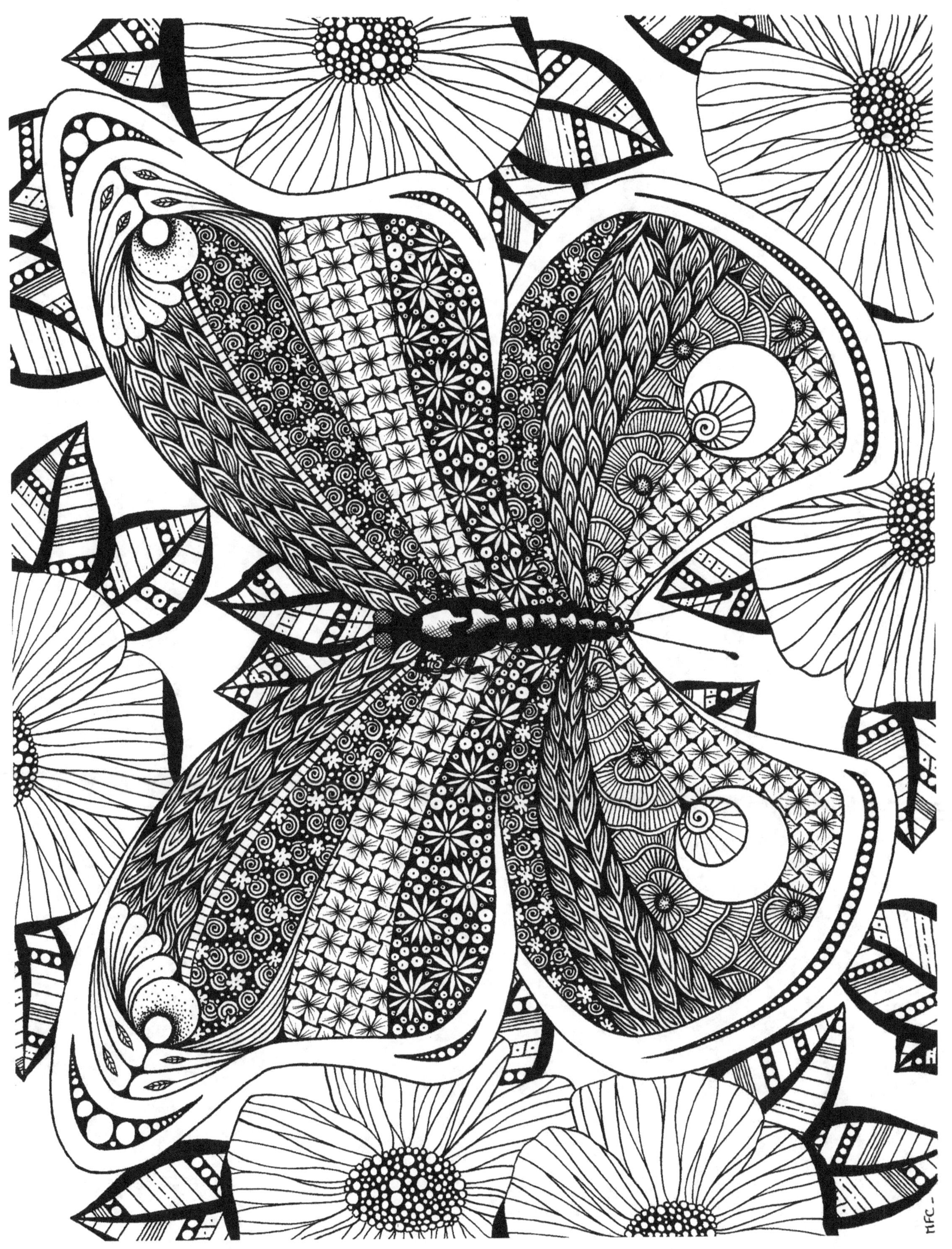

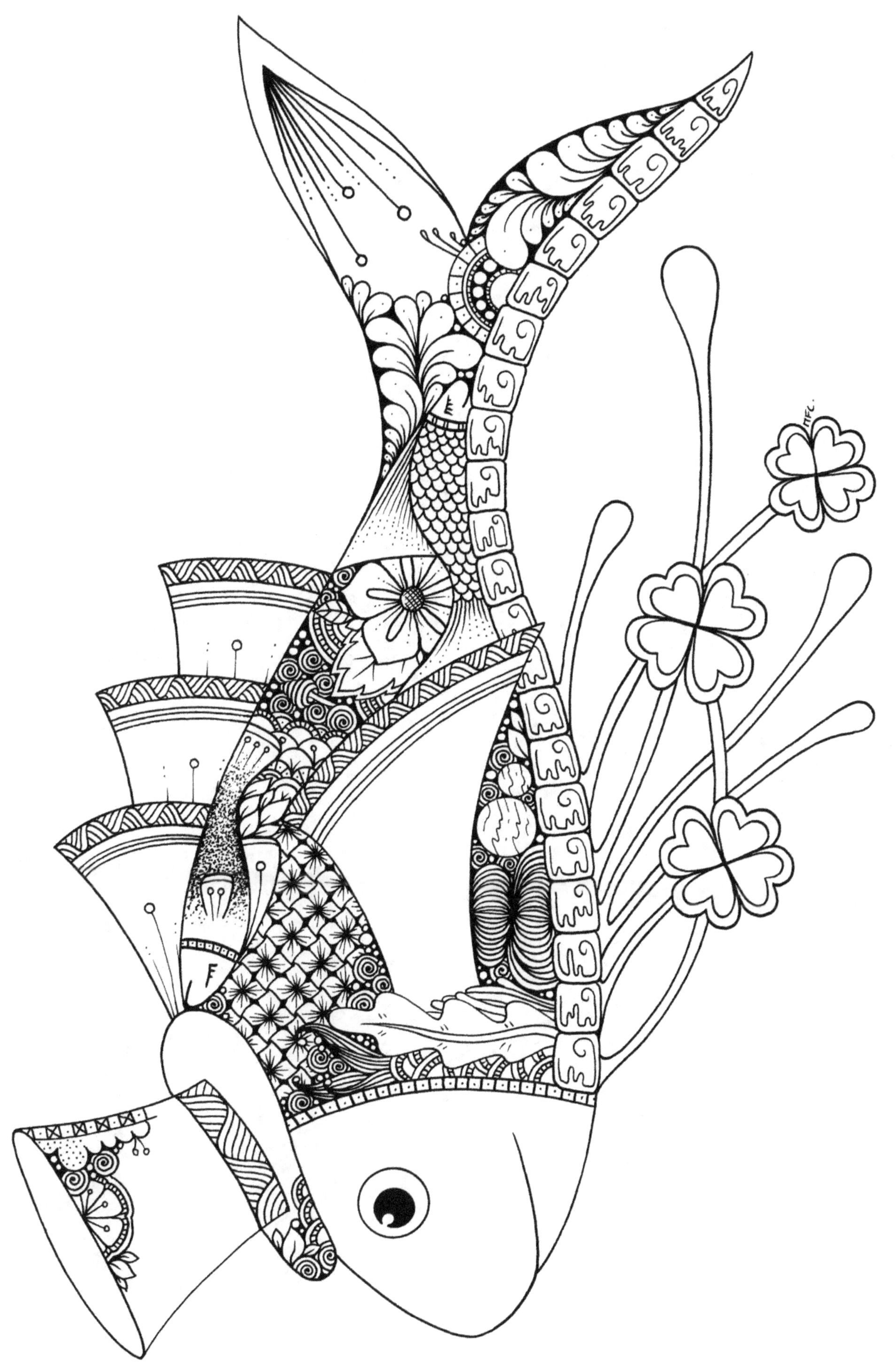

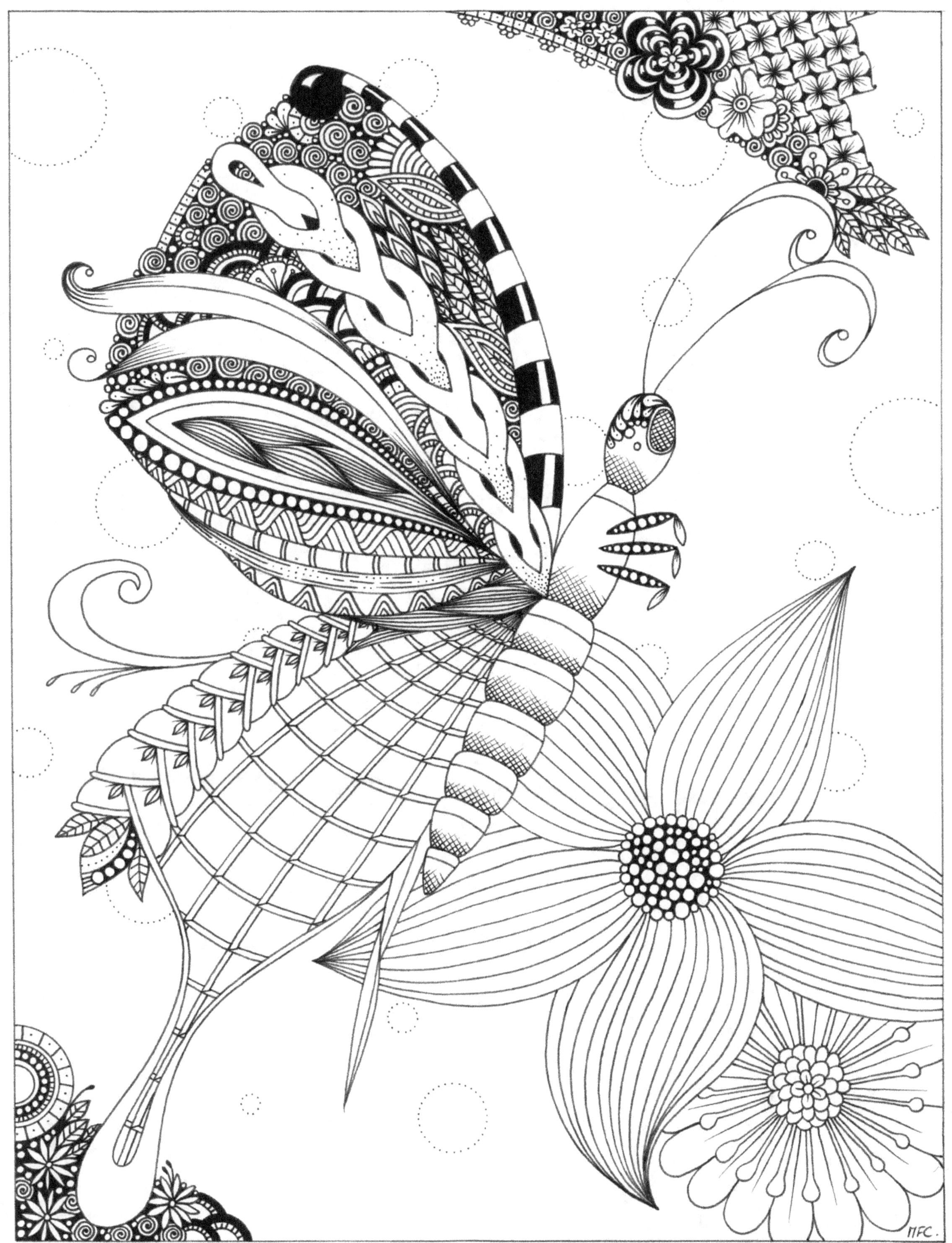

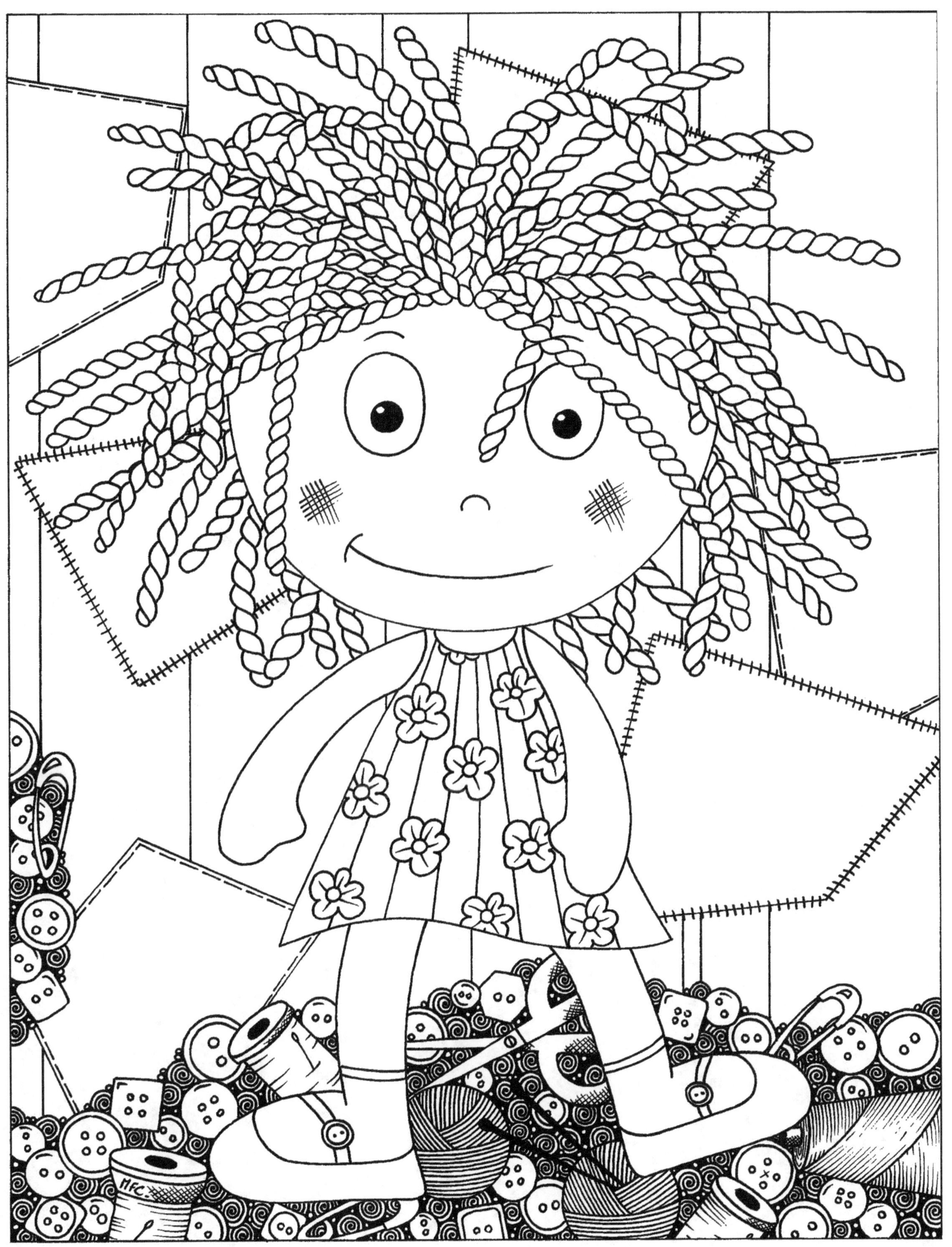

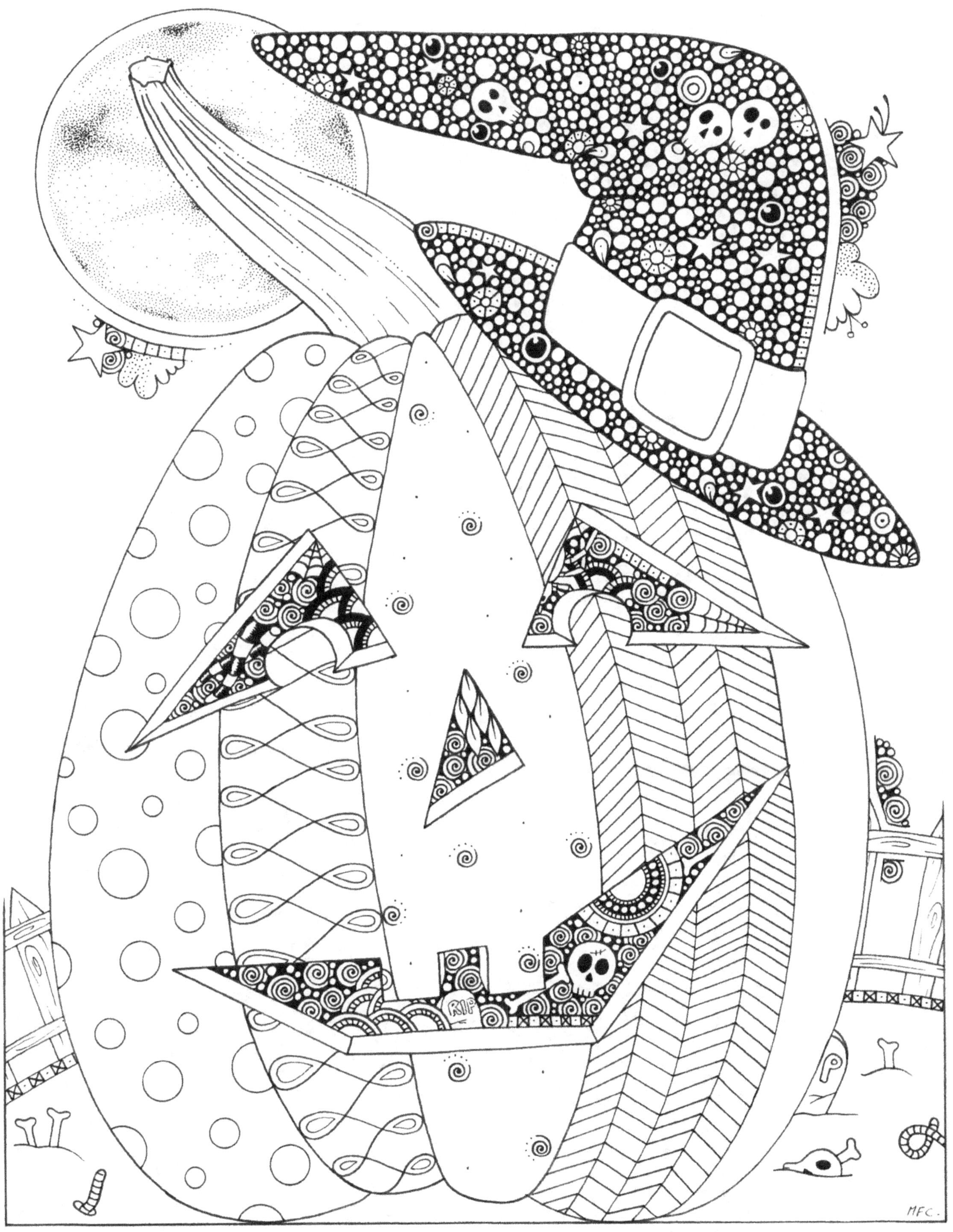

RIP
MFC.

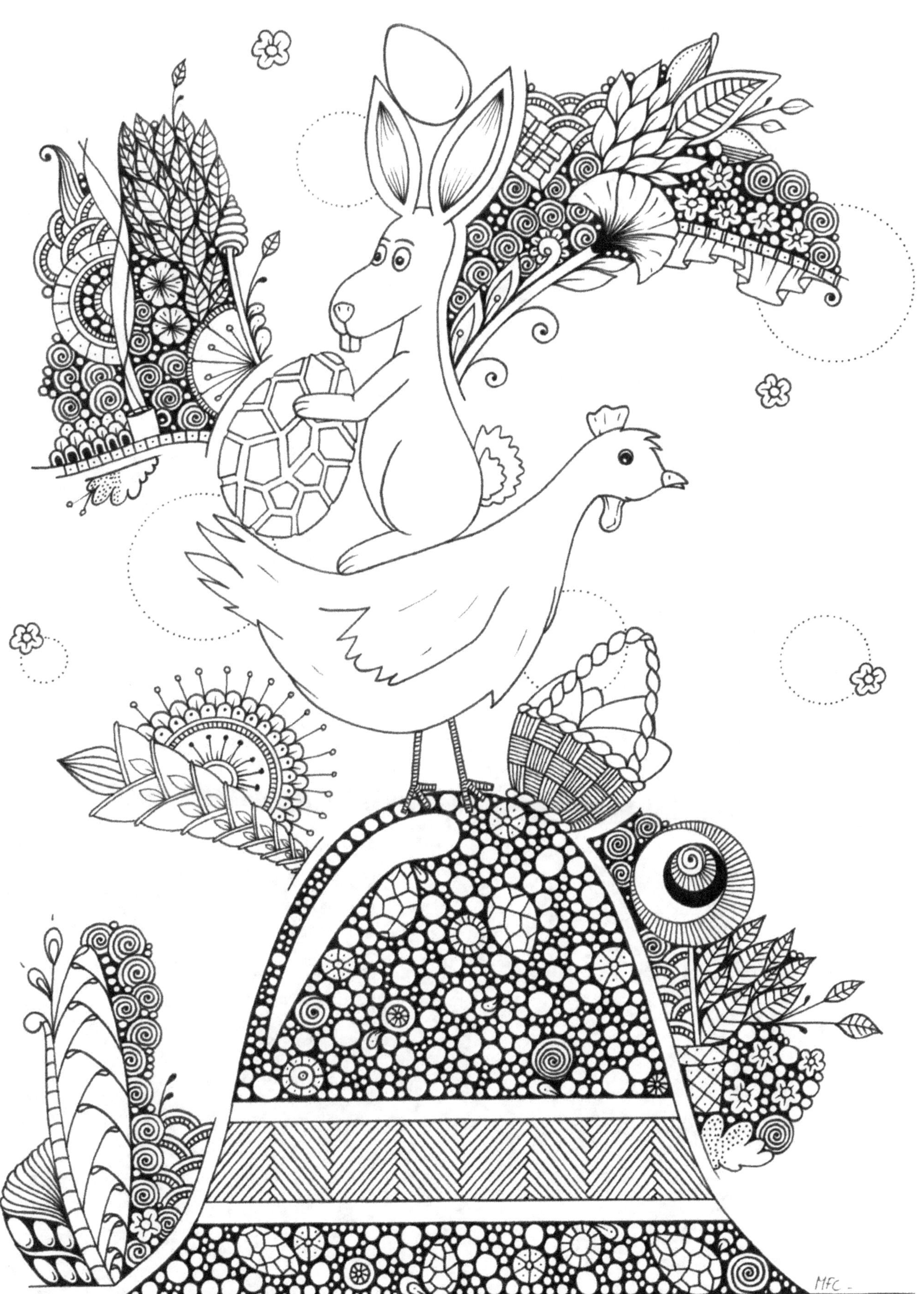
MFC

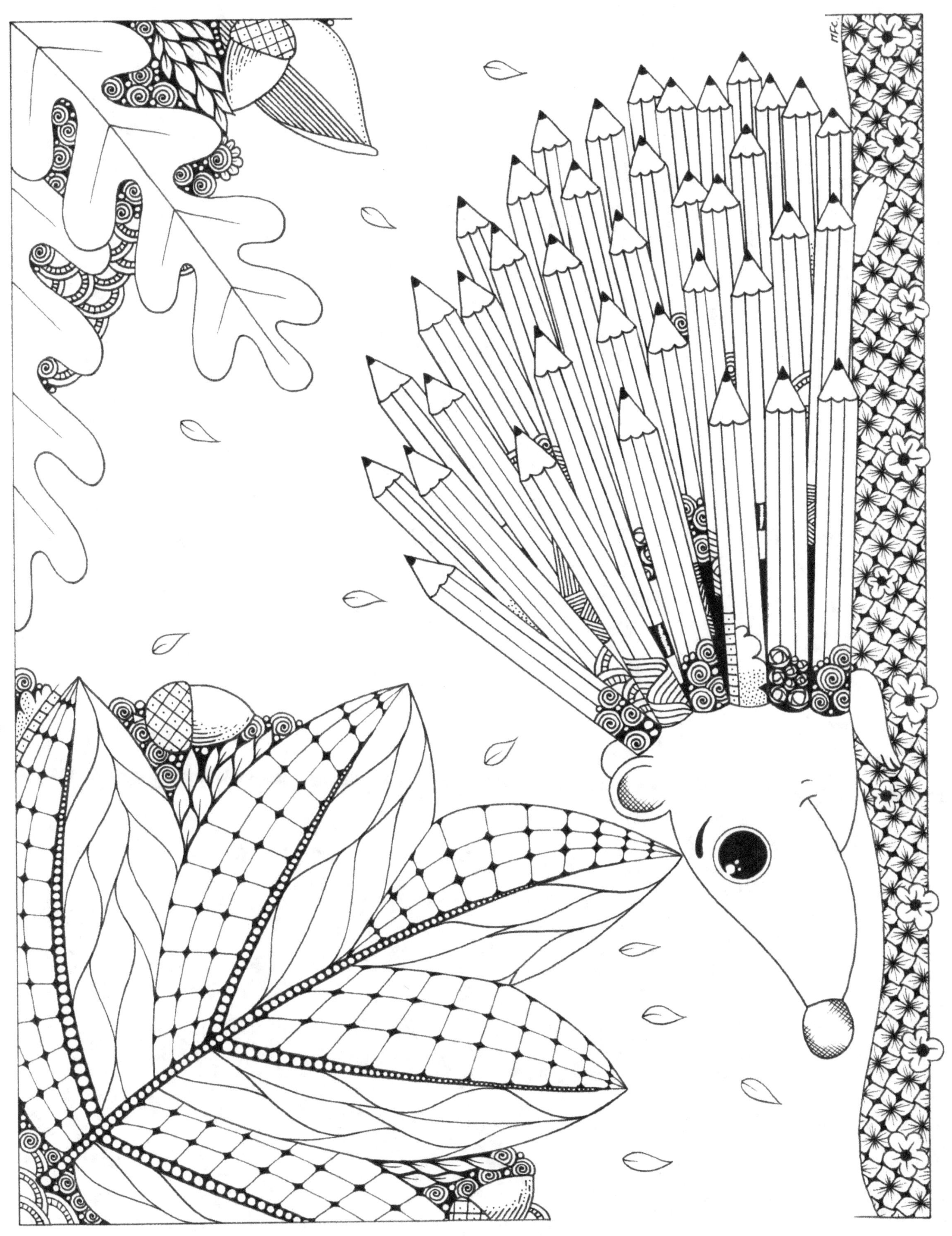

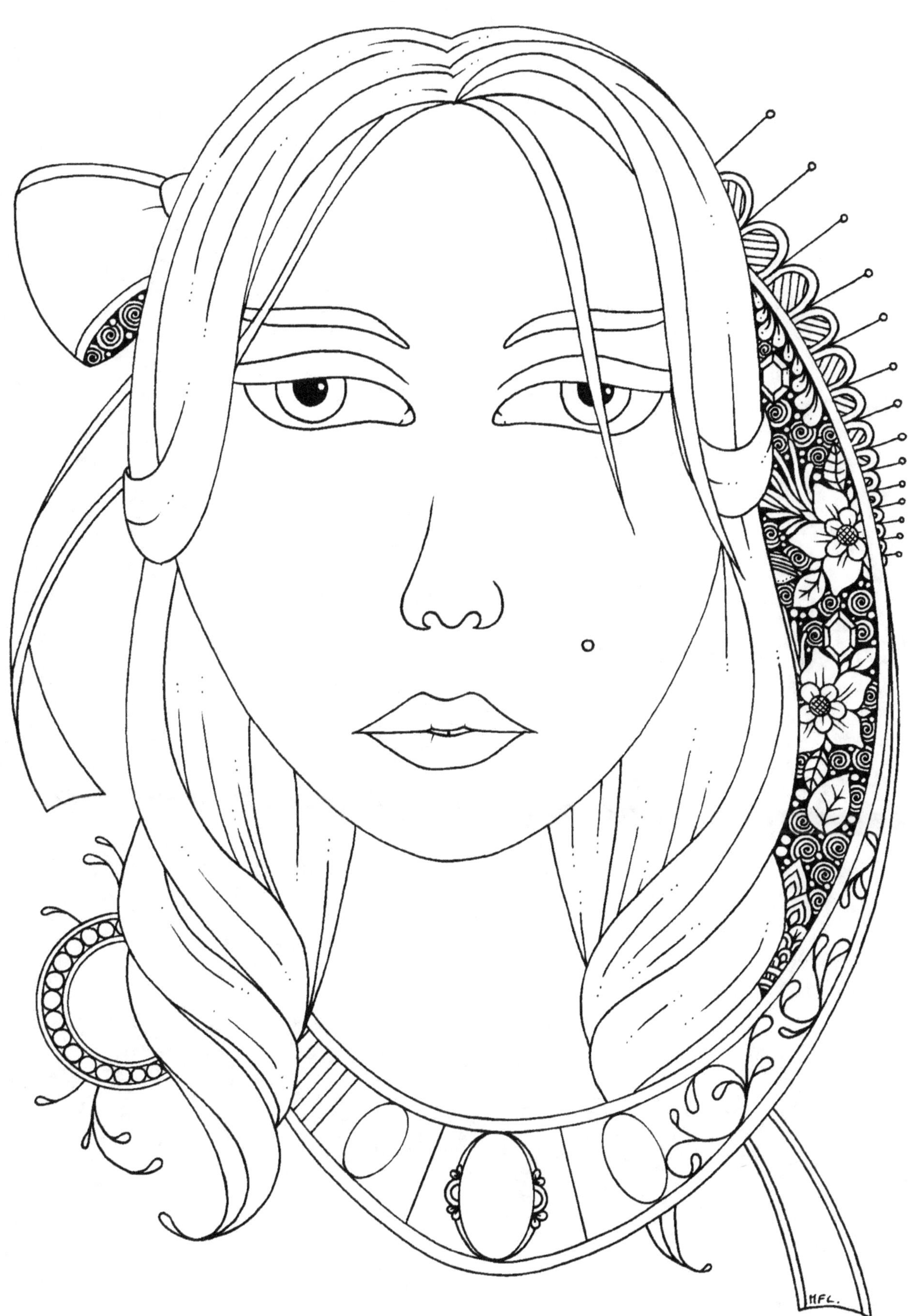

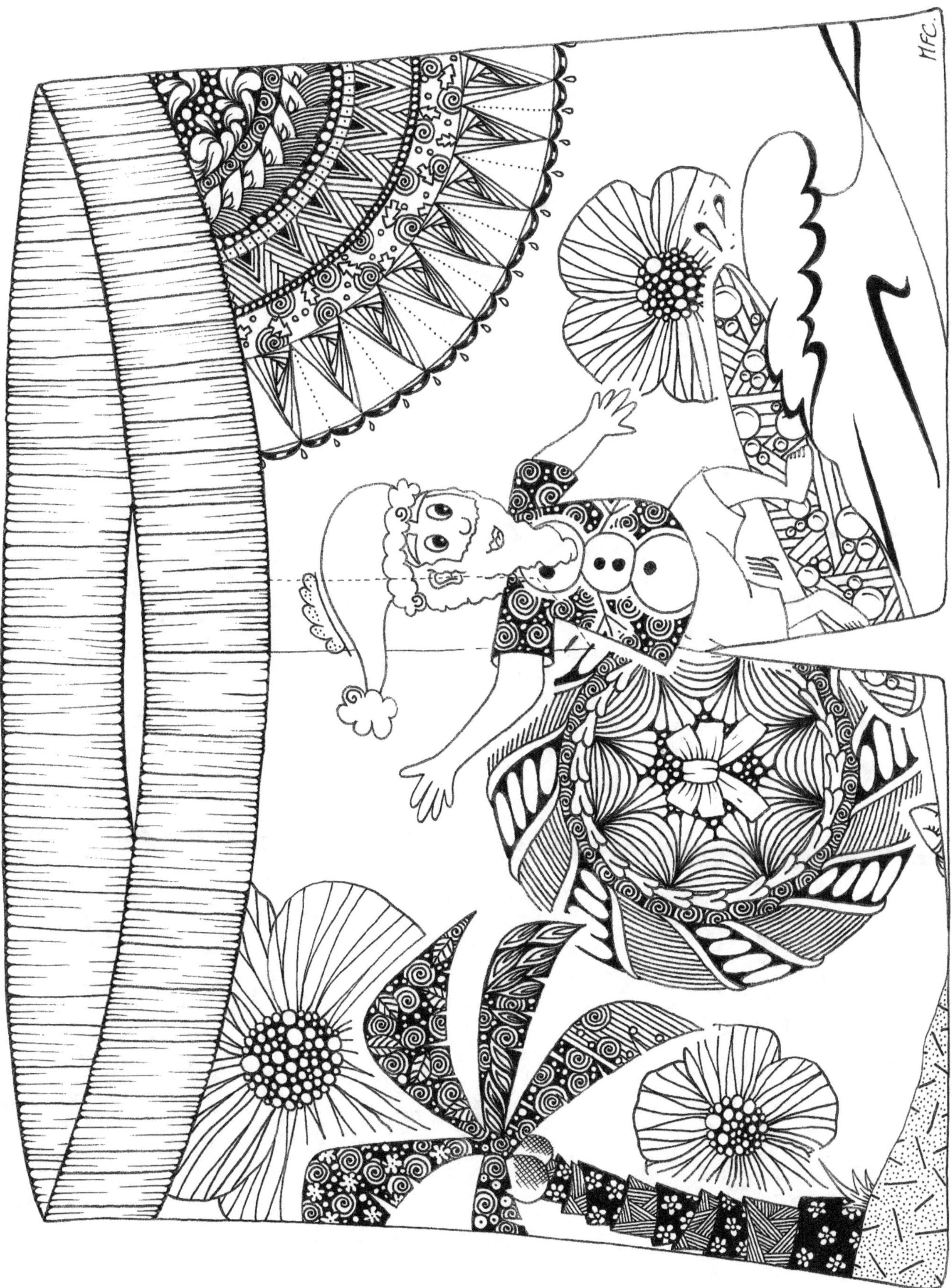

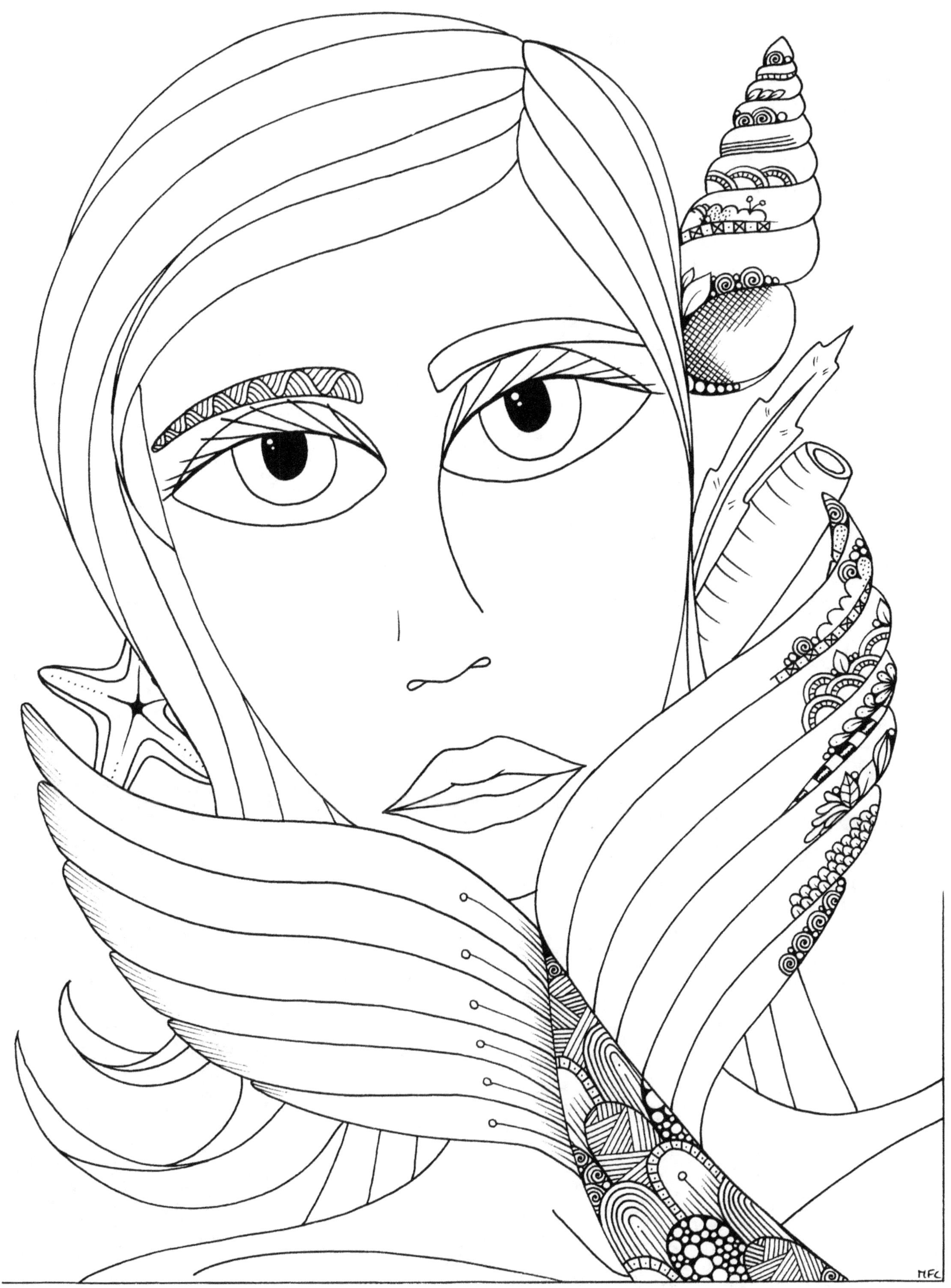

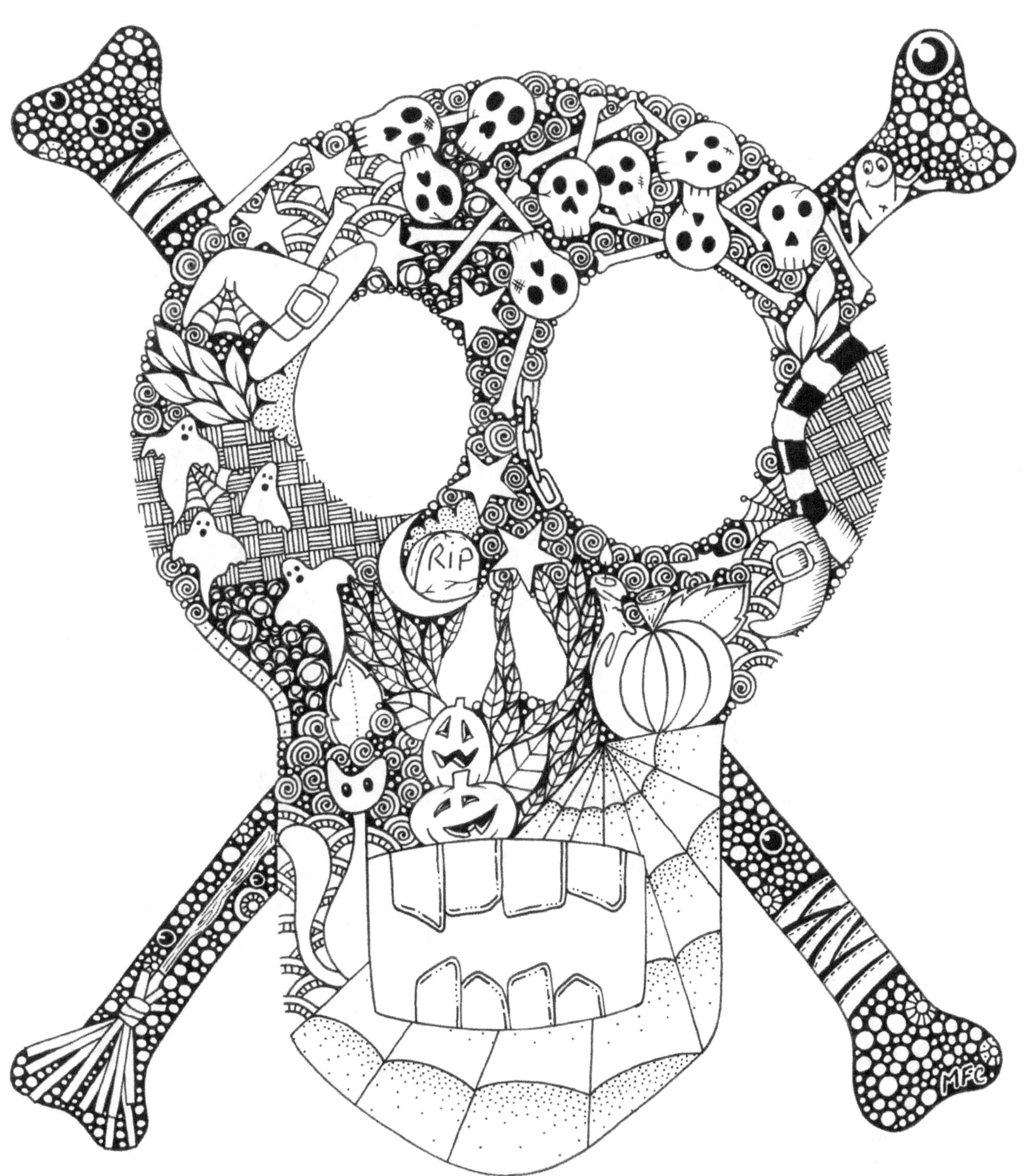

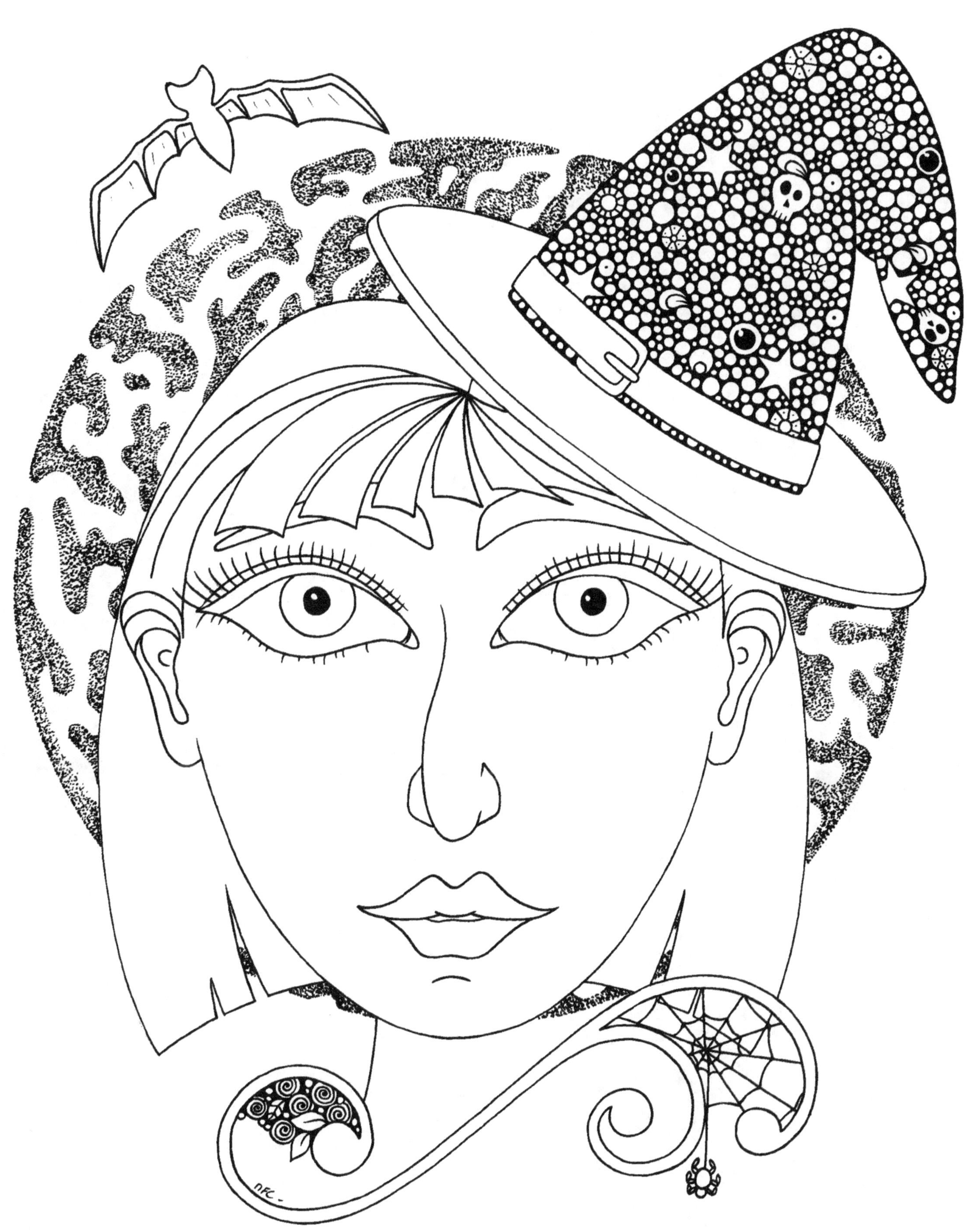

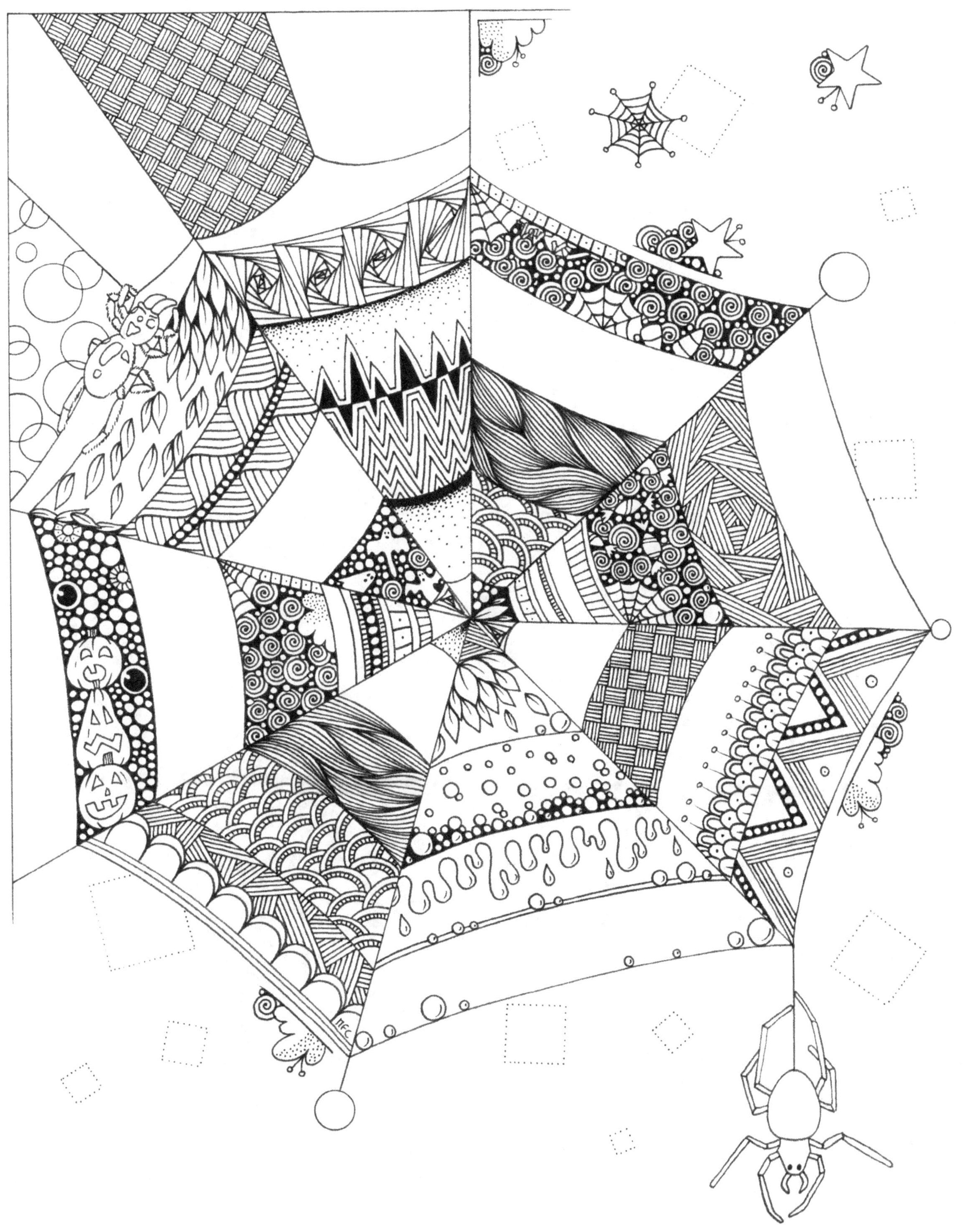

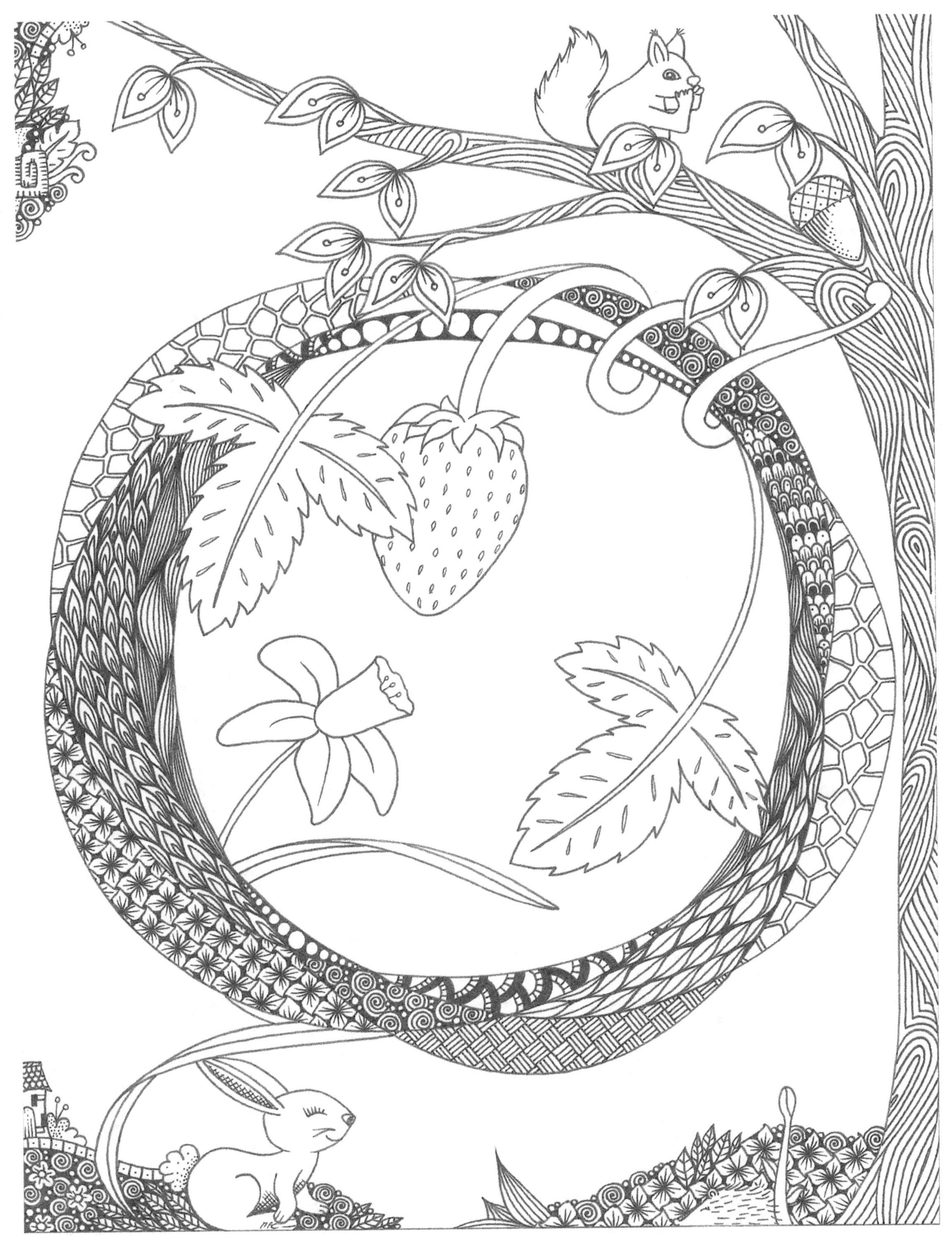

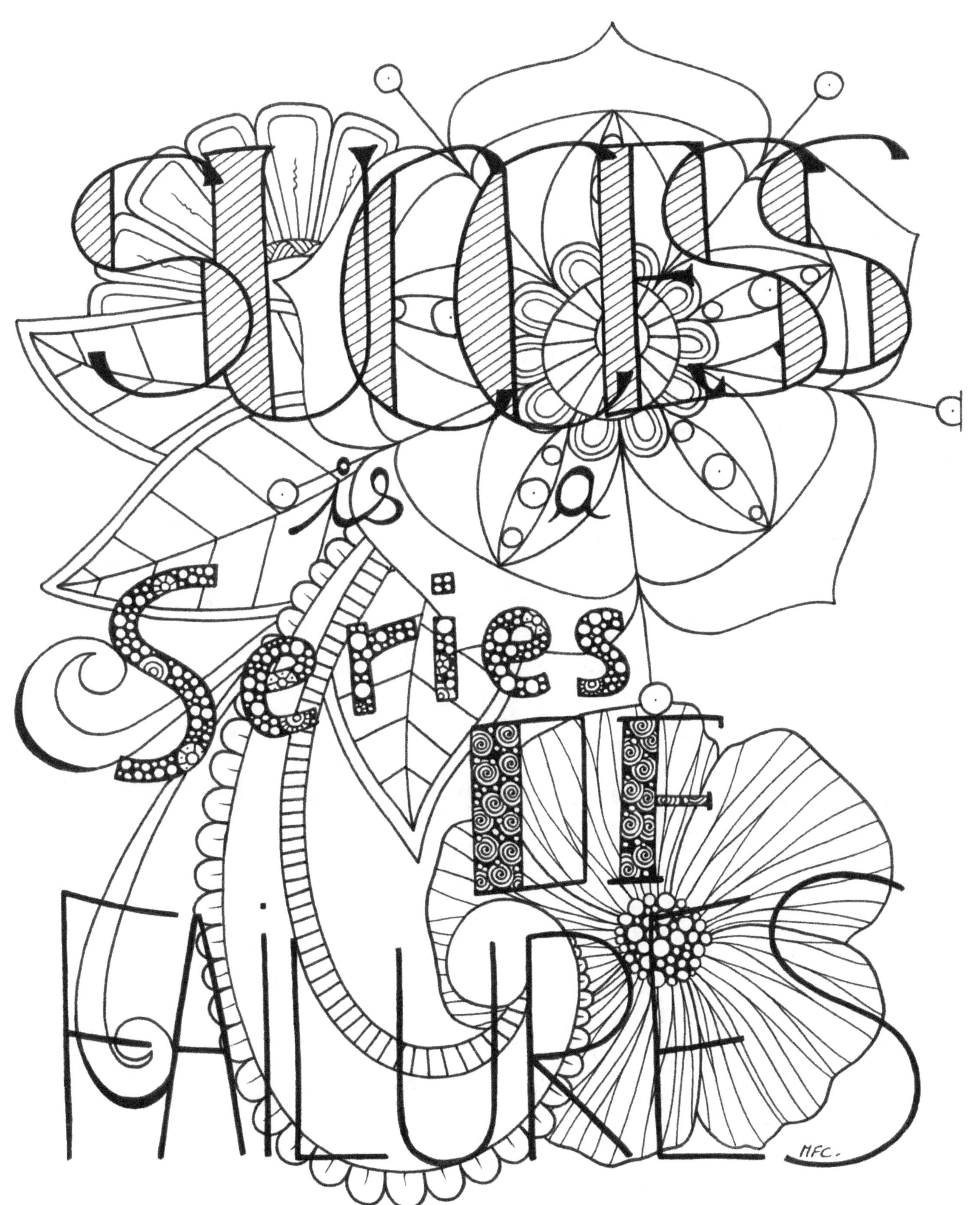

SUCCESS
is a
series
OF
FAILURES
MFC.

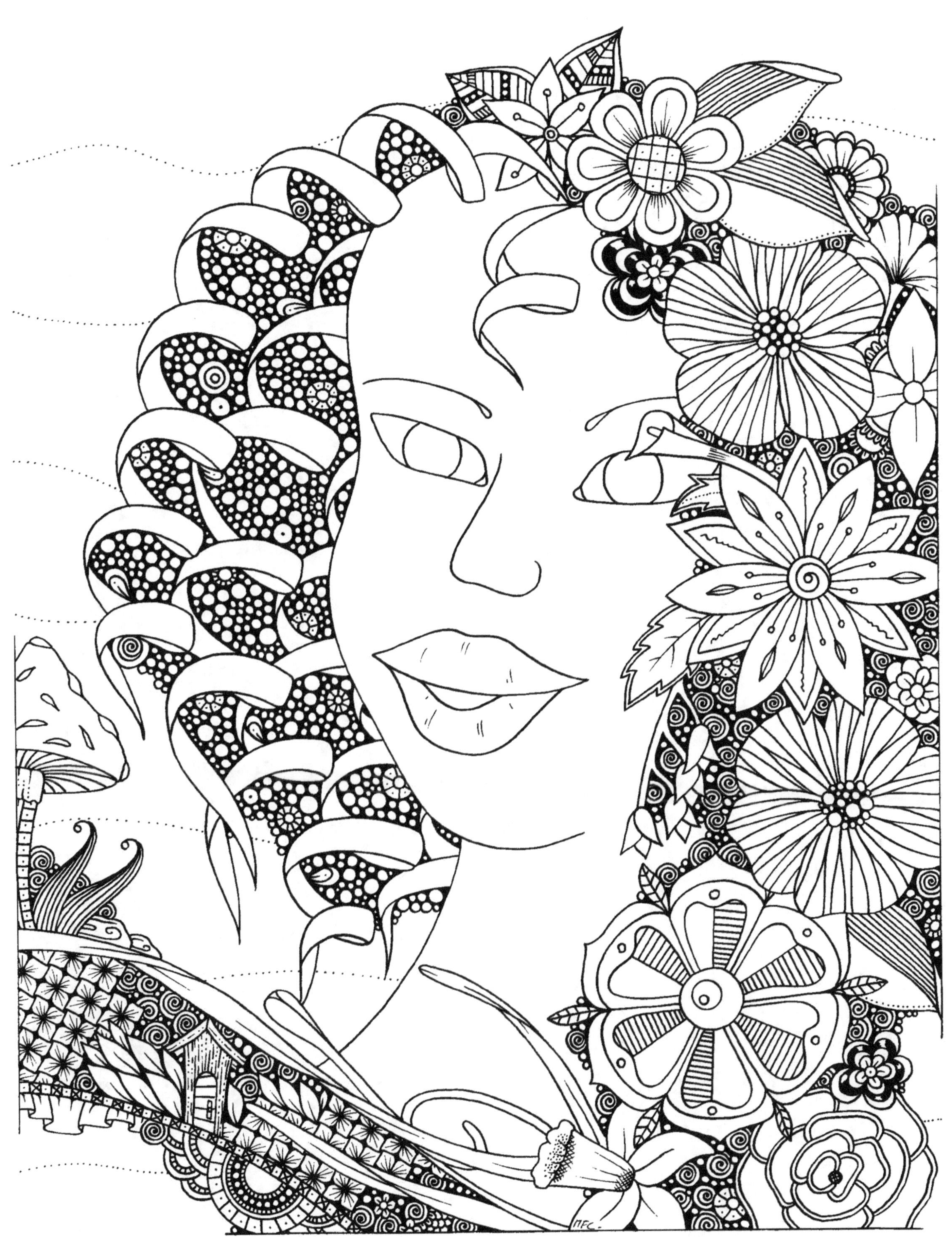

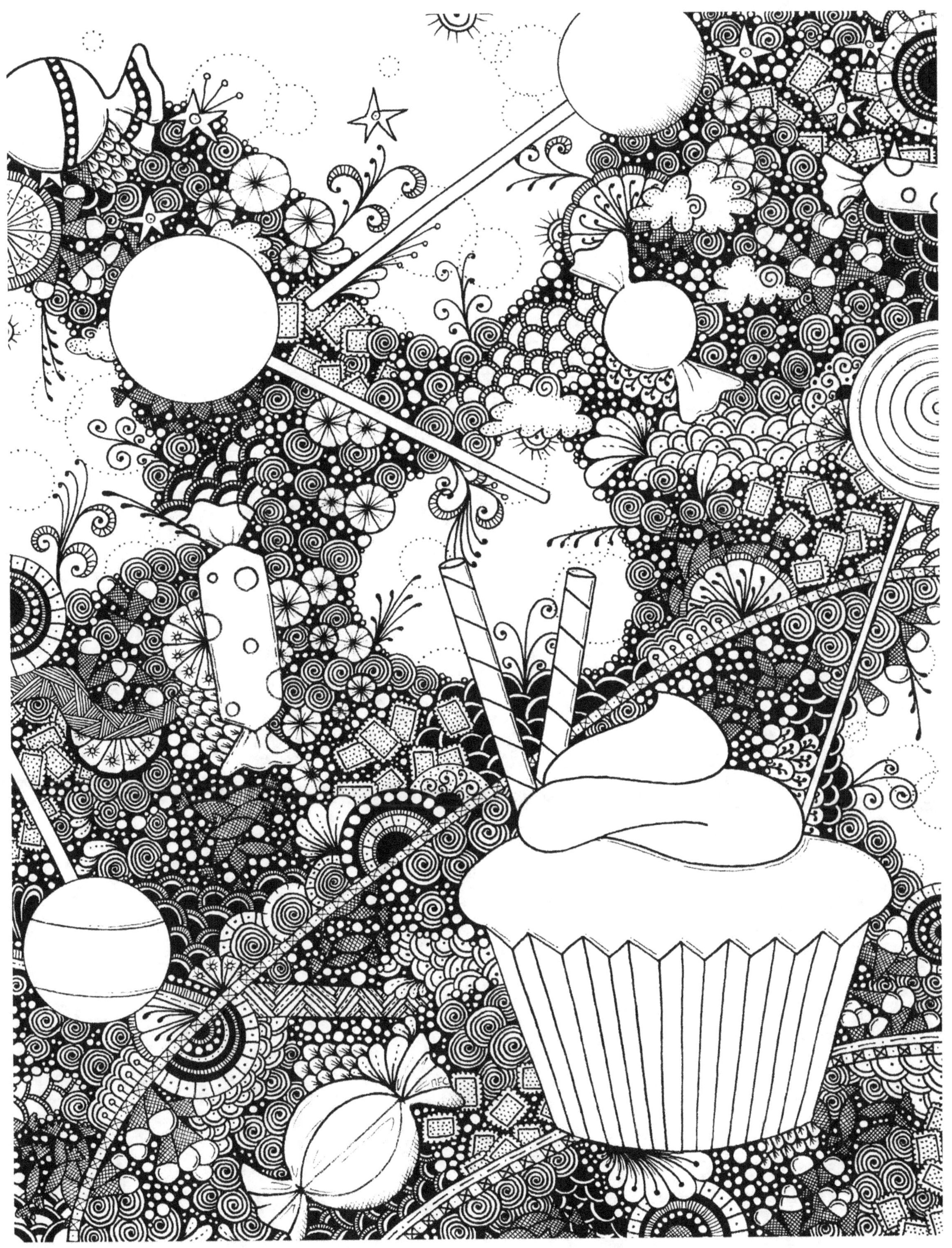

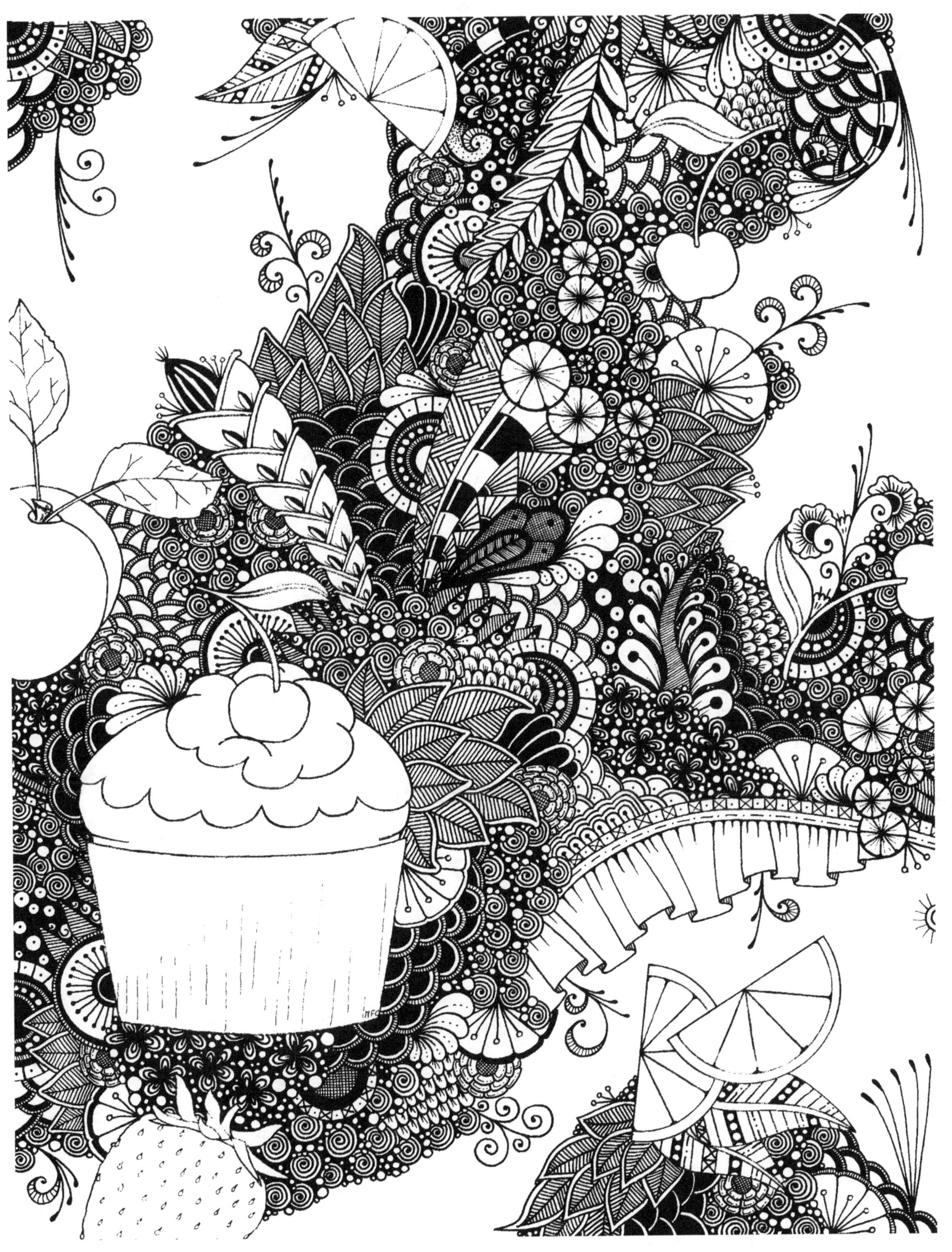

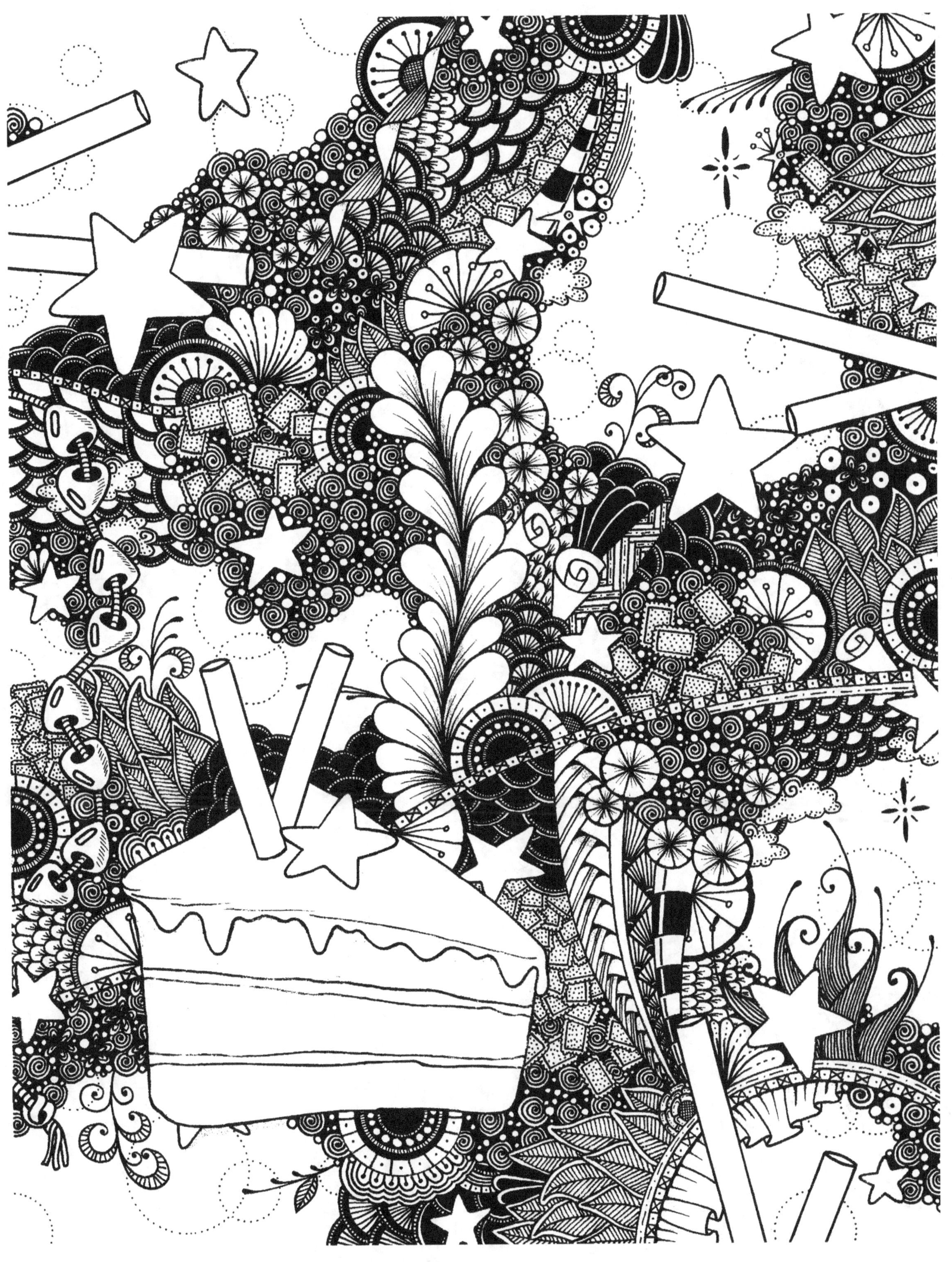

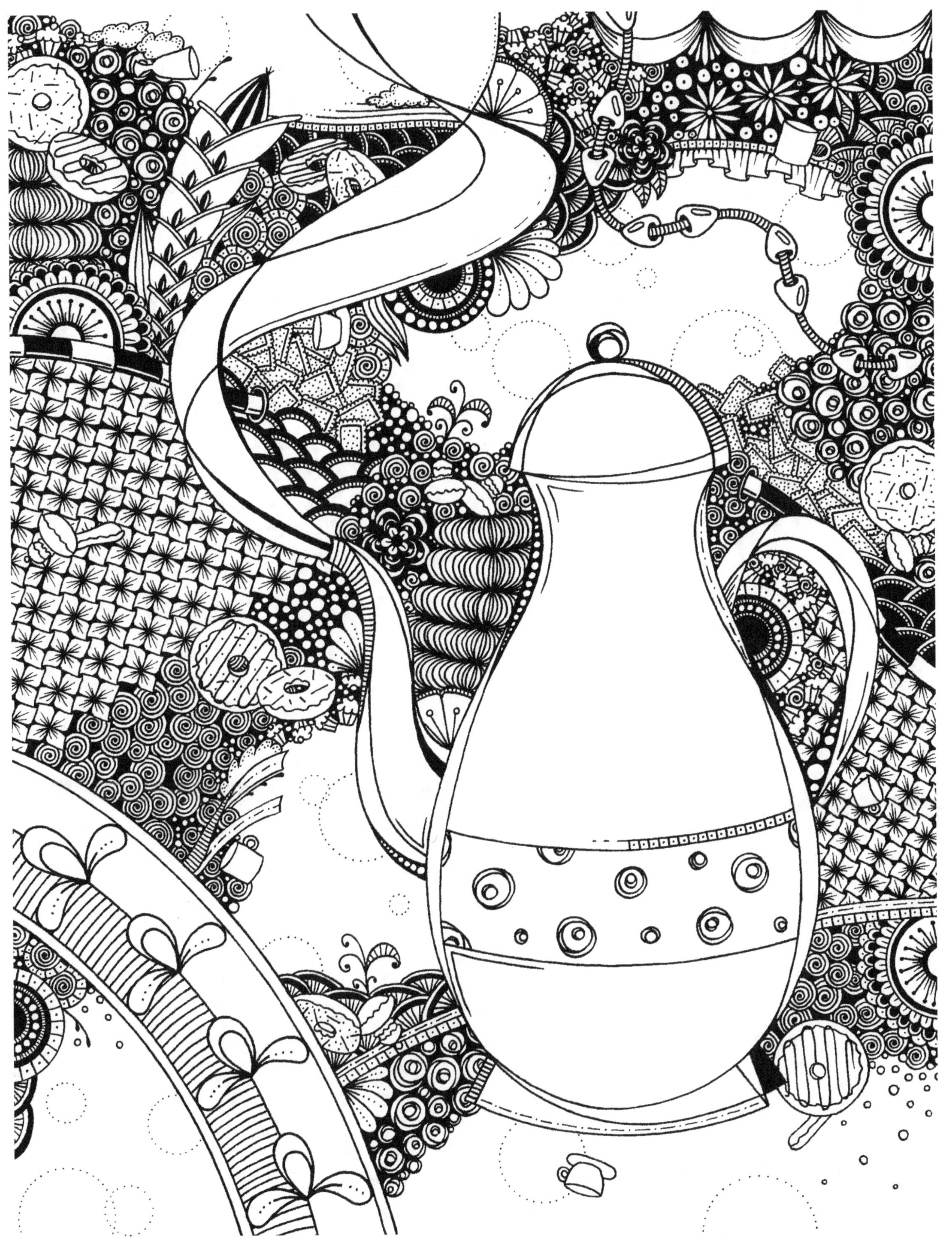

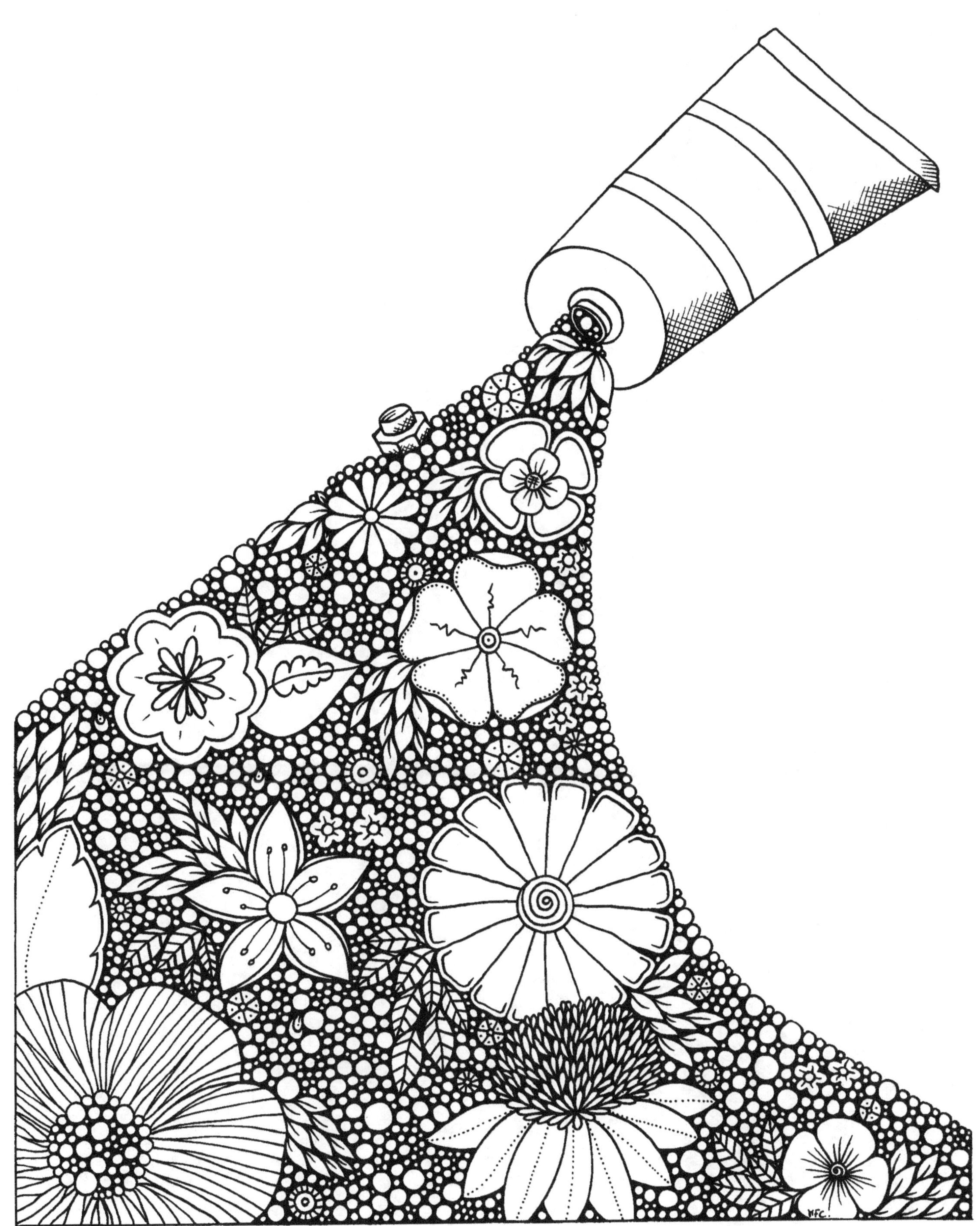

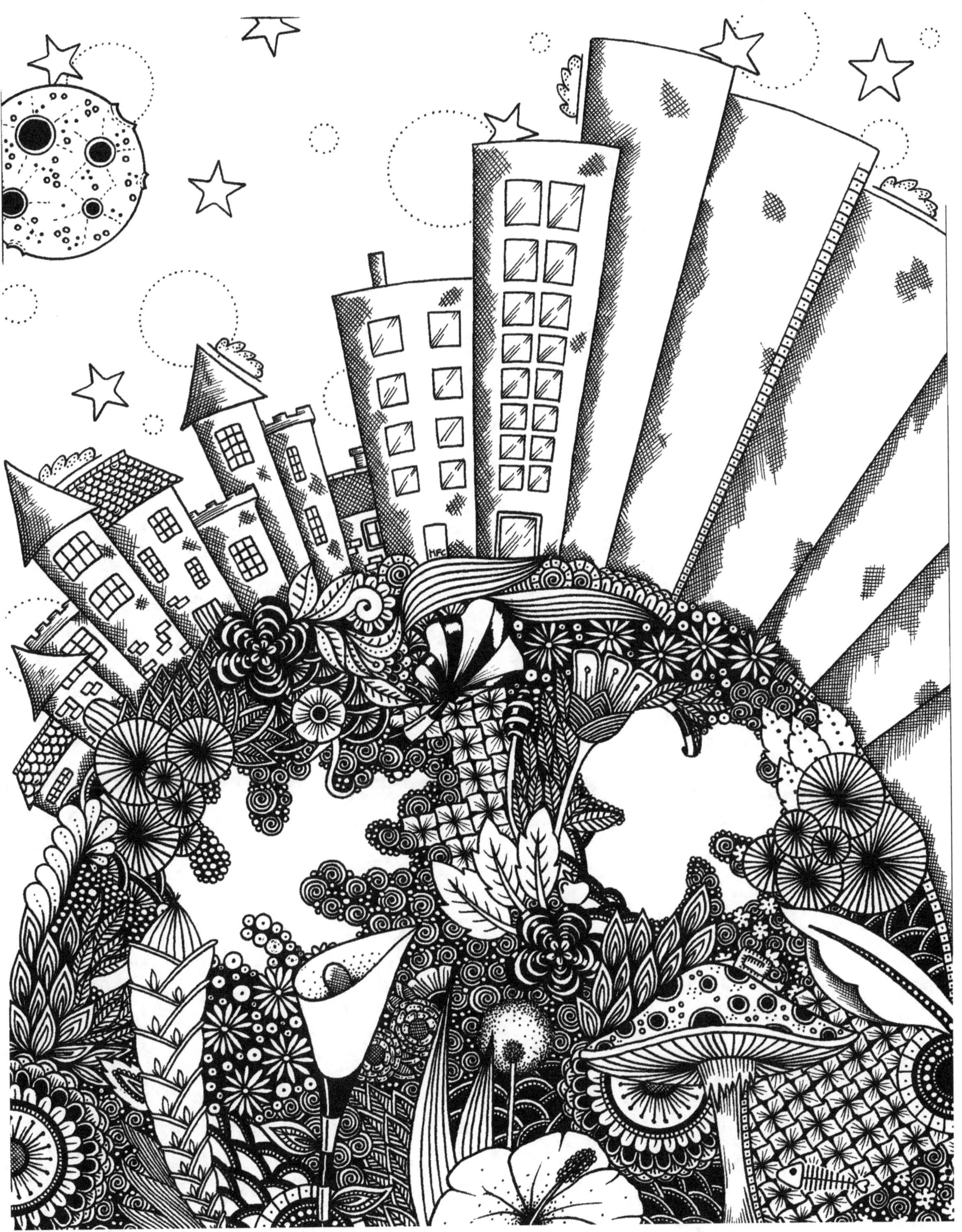

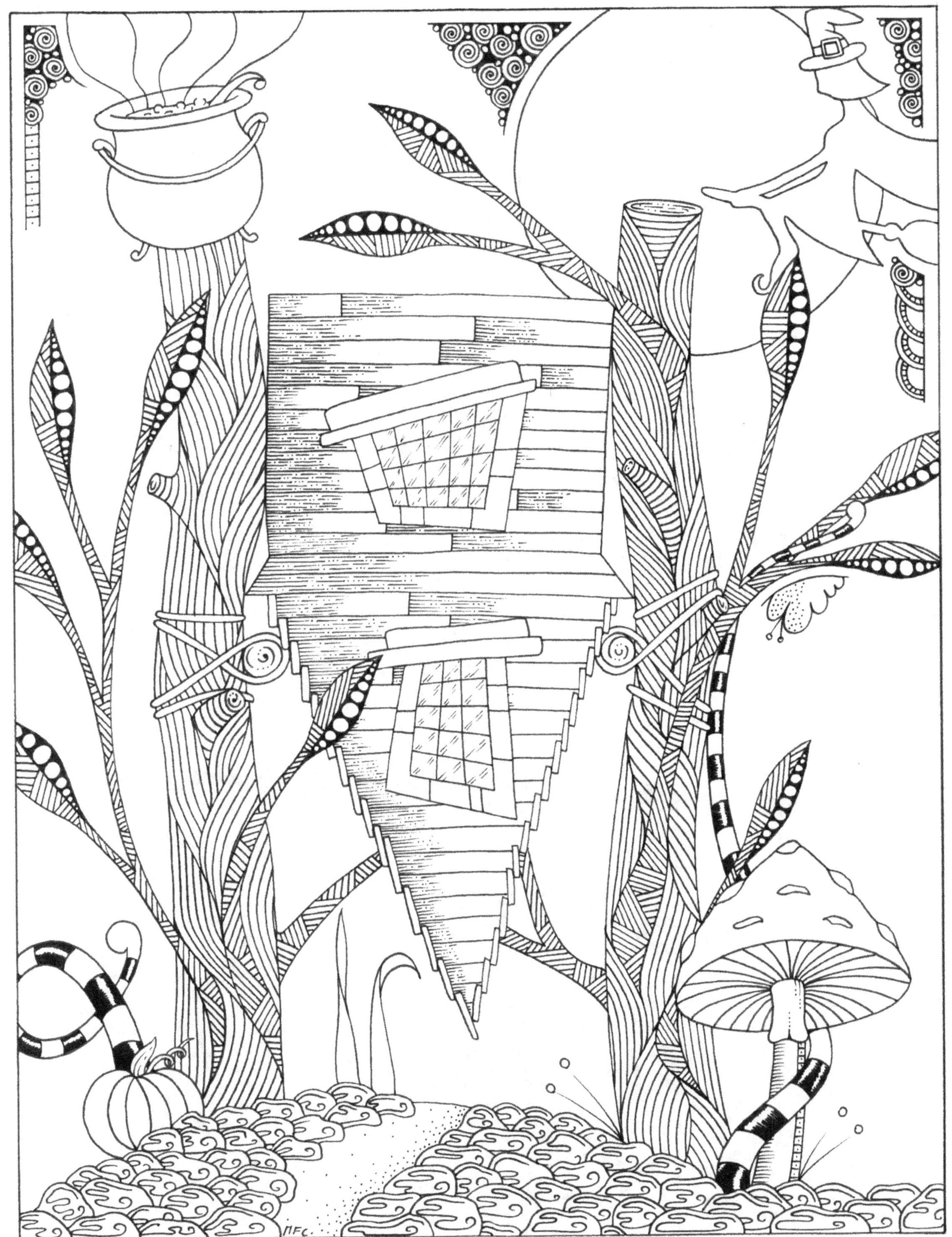

9791091517188